CRUISING THE *MISSISSIPPI*

CRUISING THE *MISSISSIPPI*

From New Orleans to Memphis on a Genuine Paddlewheeler

Al & Sunny Lockwood

FRONT PORCH PUBLISHING
MOUNTAIN HOME, NORTH CAROLINA

Cruising the Mississippi:
From New Orleans to Memphis on a genuine paddlewheeler

Published by Front Porch Publishing
Mountain Home, North Carolina

Distributed by Gatekeeper Press
2167 Stringtown Rd, Suite 109
Columbus, Ohio 43123-2989
www.GatekeeperPress.com

ISBN: 9781642370782
eISBN: 9781642370775
Library of Congress Number: 2019933988

Printed in the United States of America

OTHER TRAVEL MEMOIRS
BY AL & SUNNY LOCKWOOD

Cruising Panama's Canal
Savoring 5,000 nautical miles and 500,000 decadent calories

Cruising the Mediterranean
From the luminous canals of Amsterdam and Venice to the stunning mosaics of Istanbul's Blue Mosque, this travel memoir takes readers on the trip of a lifetime.

Finding Ourselves in Venice, Florence, Rome & Barcelona
Aging adventurers discover the power of place while exploring fascinating cities at their own relaxing pace.

Cruising the Atlantic
Our Epic Journey from Barcelona to Miami

CONTENTS

I haven’t been everywhere, but it’s on my list.
— Susan Sontag

People don’t take trips; trips take people.
— John Steinbeck

INTRODUCTION

If you've ever been bitten by the travel bug, you know how the idea of a trip (short or long, near or far) can set your heart a-pumping and your head a-dreaming. Just the thought of walking on ground, or pavement, or cobblestones you've never stepped on before can make you pull out the suitcases and start packing.

Sweetheart Al and I were bitten when we were kids. He was in California, eighteen, and about to board an airplane (along with many other young men in uniform) headed for Vietnam. I was twelve, growing up in Michigan in a family that enjoyed camping in Yellowstone, or the Great Smoky Mountains, or along the shores of Lake Superior.

Decades later, when Al and I met, we were delighted to find we'd both been to

Prague, Czechoslovakia back in the 1990s, well before it became a hot tourist destination. He was there with a group of photographers. I went with my reporter's notebook. And we both found the city, its bridges, buildings, and people life-enriching.

From the start, Sweetheart and I shared the pleasures and challenges of travel: day trips to photograph wildflowers in the Sierra Nevada Mountains, weekend trips to explore little leftover Gold Rush towns along California State Highway 49, and longer journeys to Oregon, Washington, Nevada, and Utah.

Then, on a peaceful summer evening in 2012, a car crash changed our lives. We were waiting at a red traffic light, just outside of Napa, California, when a texting driver slammed into us at full highway speed, totaling both our cars in a painful explosion of glass and metal.

Although we suffered no broken bones, we were bruised and banged up and spent most of the rest of the summer at the doctor's office or the pharmacy trying to get back to normal.

That wreck convinced us that life is fragile. And temporary. You can be doing nothing more dangerous than sitting at a red light and the next moment, you can be in the hospital, or worse, in the morgue.

That recognition changed us. We stopped putting off things we'd dreamed about. We stopped saying, "We'll do that someday" and decided to make "someday" today.

Most of our dreams were travel related. We immediately added ocean cruising to our travel repertoire. Between 2012 and 2017, we took six ocean cruises including four trans-atlantic journeys.

We wandered the crooked streets of Venice, stood awestruck on Athens' Acropolis, discovered delectable Turkish Delight in Istanbul, fell in love with enchanting Malta, photographed Gibraltar's Barbary apes, admired the architecture of Antoni Gaudi in Barcelona, searched for the home of Hans Christian Andersen in Copenhagen, saw Scotland from under our umbrellas, and shivered our way around Iceland's Golden Circle, to name a few of the fascinating places we visited.

We found cruise ship travel virtually trouble free despite our age-related limitations including heart disease and arthritic knees. The convenience of having all travel details—

transportation, lodging, entertainment, meals and snacks—handled for a package price is quite comforting. And on a cruise, you only unpack once. Though we'd spend hours on pre-trip research, as soon as we stepped aboard, we'd totally relax and simply enjoy the journey.

Over the years, we had talked about taking a river cruise along the Rhine or Danube in Europe, but the itineraries included daily hikes that took hours and required more stamina than we thought we could muster.

One afternoon, when I was just tooling around online, I stumbled upon an opportunity Al and I had never thought of: a river cruise within the United States. And not just any river, but the great Mississippi River. The industrial-strength watercourse backbone of our country.

There on my computer screen were dramatic photographs of the mighty Mississippi and of riverboats brimming with happy passengers.

"Let's take a Mississippi River cruise," I suggested. "We've learned about all kinds of European cities and countries. Let's learn a little more about our own nation."

Having spent our entire adult lives in California, we'd barely glanced at the Midwest or eastern U.S. as places to explore.

But in July 2015, we surprised ourselves by moving clear across the continent from California to western North Carolina, a five-day, 2,650-mile journey in his pickup and my car. We moved to be closer to family; my sister and her husband had retired here. The high cost of living in Sonoma County, not far from San Francisco, was another reason for our move. As retirees living on Social Security and our savings, we realized we needed to be where it cost less to live.

The Blue Ridge Mountain town we now call home captured our hearts with its picture-perfect Main Street, cozy restaurants, sweet chocolate shops and intriguing galleries. The meandering rivers and roaring waterfalls filling nearby forests have become our rejuvenators. And since we've arrived, we've immersed ourselves in the art, music, and culture of this area.

Now, staring at my computer screen filled with Mississippi River scenes, the tingle of curiosity sent me searching the internet and dreaming about a river cruise in the heart of our beloved U.S.A.

More than one company offers Mississippi cruises, but we were attracted to the American Queen Steamboat Company. Its flagship, the *American Queen*, has six decks and is a genuine steam-powered paddlewheeler. Nothing like traveling a historic river in an equally historic riverboat.

I was impressed with the fact that the *American Queen* boasts one of the most expansive collections of Tiffany glass on any boat, and that the *Guinness Book of World Records* has named it the largest riverboat ever built.

What excited us both was not only the various cruises offered by the company, but also that each cruise included a hotel room the night before boarding and a hop-on, hop-off bus tour at each stop along the paddlewheel trip.

Sweetheart and I discovered the pleasure of hop-on, hop-off buses years ago when we were visiting Washington, D.C. These tourist buses make getting from one point of interest to another easy. Passengers can hop off to explore a museum or garden or restaurant and when they're done, wait for the next bus and hop on again.

Hop is not the most accurate description for how we get on and off the bus, but for older folks like us, these buses are a godsend. When tired, we can simply sit and ride, listening to the onboard tour guide explain what we're seeing. Once we've recovered our energy, we can continue exploring.

We've ridden hop-on, hop-off buses all over Europe. The tickets can cost as little as eighteen dollars or as much as thirty-five dollars for a day's ride. And the *American Queen* has a fleet of buses waiting at each stop to give passengers an intimate view of the historic river towns along the way.

Bus passengers learn about a town's history and culture from a local onboard guide, while enjoying the freedom to explore local sights at leisure. There is no extra charge for riding these buses; they are included in the price of the cruise.

We found the Mississippi River cruises quite pricey compared to the ocean cruises we've taken. However, when we consider all that's included—

the hotel room, the hop-on, hop-off bus tours, complimentary wine and beer with dinner, and complimentary designer coffees throughout the day—the higher cost feels a bit more comfortable. Also, the cruise line pays all entrance fees to museums and other sights along the bus routes.

And on top of all that, we'll be traveling on a beautiful historic boat with far fewer passengers than an ocean liner. Most ocean cruises we've taken involved a thousand passengers or more. Our transatlantic cruises carried almost four thousand passengers. The *American Queen*, by contrast, has room for about four hundred passengers.

The more we explored the possibility, the more enthralled we became. We decided on an inside cabin (the least expensive cabins on any cruise).

We called the cruise phone number and also had our travel agent give them a call with additional questions. After getting our questions answered, we registered for a December 13 to 20 cruise from New Orleans to Memphis. The theme of our cruise was "Holiday—Christmas Markets."

Because of the time of year, I suspected we wouldn't have the best weather, so we packed sweaters, coats, and other warm clothes.

"Think chilly, rainy, maybe even some snow," I warned Al.

"I'm thinking warm from the oven cookies every afternoon," he replied with a grin. His online menu research had convinced him that he'd have no trouble snacking on fresh desserts whenever he felt the urge.

We were eager to cruise on an authentic paddlewheeler on the great Mississippi, and learn about parts of America we'd never seen before.

Thank you for joining us as we cruise the mighty Mississippi from New Orleans to Memphis on a genuine paddlewheeler.

The *American Queen* parked at Nottoway Plantation, the South's largest antebellum mansion and one of the stops on our cruise.

AL'S ANTICIPATION OF OUR FIRST RIVER CRUISE

Even though I'm a seasoned veteran of ocean cruising, I wasn't quite sure what to expect of the American Queen. *We've done a number of ocean-crossing trips on vessels of eighty thousand tons displacement and larger: the* Queen *displaces three thousand seven hundred tons. We're adapted (with some difficulty, to be sure) to two thousand passengers or more; the* Queen *holds four hundred thirty six.*

Would this (relatively) little paddlewheeler be a comfortable home for our voyage?

Two things about the Queen *definitely had me excited: the steam engine and the food.*

The engine is, and I quote from the company website: a "four-cylinder, horizontally inclined, tandem-piston, steeple-compounded, double-

acting reciprocating steam engine." For this mechanical engineer, such a description is the Hallelujah chorus, led by an archangel with saints doing solo verses.

The only steam engines I'd ever seen were those powering locomotives and one powering a sawmill. Substantial, though old and inefficient (me too, I must admit).

Anyway, the American Queen's *four-cylinder power plant sounds like a Swiss watch by comparison. And the best part: I can go down to the engine room and watch this marvel operate any time the boat's underway. You sure can't do that on an ocean liner! I can't wait.*

As to food, I assume that the American Queen *doesn't serve casseroles. More important to my palate is the ready availability of desserts on the paddlewheeler.*

I have a distinct predilection for sweets, both at and between meals. As Ernestine Ulmer has said, "Life is uncertain: eat dessert first."

I say, eat dessert first. And often, if possible. To my delight, American Queen's *website promises 24/7 cookies and a serve-it-yourself soft ice cream dispenser. Chocolate or vanilla or both, cone or dish. I'm ready to embark.*

OUR NIGHT IN NEW ORLEANS

I'm a fan of uneventful airplane rides and boring taxi drives. I find ordinary transportation from point A to point B restful and reassuring when I'm starting a travel adventure.

Ours is an uneventful flight from Atlanta to New Orleans, and an equally forgettable taxi ride to the Hilton Riverside on Poydras Street. But all ordinariness ends at the hotel, which is large and nestled against the banks of the Mississippi in the Warehouse and Arts District.

Receiving our room key at the front desk, we head for room 3083. As we enter, a paddlewheeler floats past our wall-size window, red paddle wheel spinning, white decks shining, flags flying atop.

Grabbing our cameras, we try to capture the image of historic beauty.

"We sure couldn't get any closer to the Mississippi River, could we?" Al says as we click away.

After the boat sporting the name *Natchez* passes, we gaze out at the waters of the Mississippi. It's almost as if we're actually in the river. Our room is that close. Great views!

And just think how the water we're staring at flowed through at least ten states: Minnesota (where the headwaters begin), Wisconsin, Iowa, Illinois, Missouri, Kentucky, Tennessee, Arkansas, Mississippi and Louisiana. More than two thousand miles of America's lifeblood.

Here we are, watching the second-largest river in the nation flow past. This is the river Samuel Clemens navigated as a steamboat pilot, the river Huck Finn and Jim traveled in their search for freedom, the river down which a teenaged Abe Lincoln guided a flatboat, and three decades later, as an attorney, supported building railroad bridges across it.

Tomorrow we'll begin to get acquainted much more personally with this vital waterway.

Today, however, we're eager to explore New Orleans.

On our way out, we stop by the American Queen Steamboat Company hospitality desk for a little orientation. The desk is set up in a large, welcoming space. Tall posters of the *American Queen* stand at both ends of the desk, and the two women in uniform behind the desk seem happy to answer our questions.

They show us where breakfast will be served tomorrow, tell us what time we need to board the boat, and invite us to sign up for an all-day city tour with local guides. It's a bus tour with a few important stops. At the end of the tour, we'll be delivered to the boat, and will be able to board without delay. By signing up for the tour, we'll also be able to register and take advantage of priority check-in tomorrow morning. At sixty-five dollars each, we're happy to sign up.

Then out we go into the late afternoon sunlight. In this warm, southern air there's no need for a sweater.

From the water's edge, the river is big, powerful, and bustling with activity. It's always been a working river, and it remains such. For the few minutes we watch, we can see tugs and tankers as well as colorful paddlewheel cruise boats all on their busy errands. Vestiges of the river's industrial past stand along the banks in the form of aging (or repurposed) warehouses and wharves.

The water here is incredibly muddy. So brown and dirty that no one in his (or her) right mind would try to swim in this toxic brew of factory poisons, pesticide and fertilizer runoff from Midwest farms, as well as oil and fuel from all the ships on their way through to the Gulf.

Still, there is a brawny beauty to the flow that's almost mesmerizing.

We turn from the busy river.

Al's never been to New Orleans before. I've been here twice. All my memories are of the French Quarter, the city's oldest neighborhood: narrow streets, balconies of intricate ironwork, and boisterous voices or lusty music tumbling out of every doorway.

My favorite memory is of the traditional New Orleans jazz concert I heard at Preservation Hall on St. Peter Street. Tonight we'll be there. Al bought *Big Shot* tickets online so we'd be guaranteed a seat.

But right now, while it's still light out, we're wandering the local neighborhood, admiring Christmas decorations and keeping our eyes peeled for a good place to eat supper.

It's Saturday and the streets are bursting with families. Little girls in tiaras and princess gowns skip through miniature Christmas tree forests. Little boys dressed like cowboys or sporting Superman capes run pell-mell here and there, while parents struggle to keep up.

Six tall, stunning black women adorned with red vests and strings of tiny blinking lights rush by in a flash of laughter. Santas are everywhere—tall, short, fat, thin, young, old—wandering among the crowds. The glitzy, joyous atmosphere wraps us up in its enthusiastic embrace.

Al glances my way, his face glowing. "I've never seen anything like this."

"Me neither!"

A side street beckons, and we walk through tunnels of blue and purple lighting.

"It's like a fairy land," I say.

Al nods.

When we spot Cafe Adelaide & the Swizzle Stick Bar, we settle at an outside table. From here we can watch the crowds while enjoying our meal. Al orders a grilled gulf shrimp plate. I have a beef po-boy, a New Orleans classic. Both meals are delicious.

Two white women in crisp, white tutus and black top hats, their faces all made up like feminine clowns, take a nearby seat. They study their phones for a few minutes. When one glances my way, I ask, "What's with all the Santas?"

"There was a Santa run today. It's an annual event," she says. "The city's full of them."

I nod. That explains it.

We savor our meal and our view. Eventually, well after dark, we return to our hotel room.

The tickets for tonight's Preservation Hall concert are for eight o'clock. We slip them in our pockets and head back outside. The French Quarter is within walking distance, but we don't like walking after dark in an unfamiliar area, so we pay ten dollars for a taxi to take us to Preservation Hall.

"I can only get you within a block or so," the driver says, inching through the crowds. "Too many people out tonight."

"Just point us in the right direction," Al says as we climb out.

The crush of bodies, many in bizarre costumes, swarm the sidewalks and street, pressing so tightly that we move glacier-like, bumping and jostling one another as we walk. No wonder the taxi couldn't get us through.

Despite the lights from restaurants, clubs, and other businesses, the night air is dark, thick, and humid. Buildings on both sides seem to lean toward the street, adding to the squeezed-together feeling.

When we arrive at the modest wrought iron entrance gate of Preservation Hall, there's already a line more than two blocks long. Thank goodness Al bought tickets online. The place is just as I remember it—unassuming to the max. If you weren't paying attention, weren't carefully searching for an address or a sign, you'd walk right past and never know it.

Above the wrought iron entrance gate hang two battered instrument cases with brass letters spelling Preservation Hall. In the darkness, this sign is next to invisible. Below it stands a woman with a clipboard. I ask if the line is for people who already have tickets.

She says it's for people hoping to get a seat at one of tonight's concerts. Then she asks, "Do you have reservations?"

Al quickly says, "We do indeed," and shows her the receipt for two bench seats. She checks our names off a sheet on her clipboard and says to come back at seven-thirty when the doors will open. Our concert starts at eight o'clock.

The dense darkness is spicy and exciting as we wander a few blocks from the hall.

This street and all the side streets are lined with clubs and restaurants, cafes and stores and they're all open and full of people. Rev. Zombie's Voodoo Shop grabs Al's attention. I lean against a wall and wait while he goes inside. When he returns, he says, "Dolls, T-shirts and hoodies, oils and herbs, and evil eye charms like the one I bought in Greece."

He was so taken by the dark blue evil eye charms that he saw in all the tourist trinket shops in Greece when we were there that he finally bought one and brought it home. It now hangs in his backyard darkroom.

We return to Preservation Hall and are first when the gate opens. In we go, eager to claim our space on a narrow, wooden, backless bench.

Hall is probably not the most accurate word to describe this thirty-one foot by twenty foot chamber of worn floor boards and crumbling plaster walls. Once an art gallery, and before that a tavern, the atmosphere of this jazz lover's Mecca is best described as no atmosphere.

Here are some other no's that make Preservation Hall unique: there is no stage; there are no microphones or speakers; there's no air conditioning. There is no bar, no bathroom, no smoking is allowed, and, as I can attest from personal experience, no comfortable seats. And in all the corners hang dusty cobwebs.

But, believe me, once the music starts, none of that matters.

Four rows of backless benches hold middle-aged or older folks. On the floor in front of the benches are two rows of rather threadbare cushions. Behind the benches it's standing room only.

The room fills quickly.

Al and I are only about seven feet from where the musicians will play. The college kids on the cushions in front of us are about two feet from the performance area.

At the front of the room stand five straight-backed wooden chairs, a bass drum sporting the words "Preservation Hall All Stars" in bold red letters, and an upright piano.

Chatter fills the room. Everyone's talking about their thrill in being here. How they've dreamed about this for years. How excited they are to actually be in Preservation Hall. I share the eager anticipation.

When I was here in the early 1970s, standing in the crush behind the benches, an elderly Sweet Emma Barrett—the piano player who founded the Preservation Hall Jazz Band in 1961—was still leading the group. She'd had a stroke, and her right side seemed to be paralyzed. But her left hand commanded the keyboard with power and enthusiasm. And the songs: "Basin Street Blues," "Clarinet Marmalade," and others pranced their way into my heart.

At the end of that concert, I bought the album *New Orleans' Sweet Emma and Her Preservation Hall Jazz Band.* I played that treasured album over and over through the years, carried it with me as I moved from place to place throughout northern California, yet somewhere along the way, I lost it.

But now I'm back here in this hallowed place, eagerly waiting to once again be dazzled by traditional New Orleans jazz.

At eight, the band enters—five men and a woman.

All conversation stops.

As the musicians pick up their instruments and take their places, the trumpet player, Will Smith, introduces them: Mr. Freddie Lonzo on the trombone, Mr. Louis Ford on the clarinet (and sax), Mr. Kerry Lewis on the bass, Mr. Kerry Brown on the drums and Ms. Mari Watanabe on the piano.

And note by tantalizing note, the music begins: "Bourbon St. Parade," jazzy renditions of "Hello Dolly" and "O Christmas Tree."

I don't recognize the next medley of songs, but I tap my foot along to the intoxicating beat. Hot notes bounce off old walls, fill and thrill us until we can't keep our hands still, and the hall erupts in raucous applause and enthusiastic cheers.

Will Smith sets his trumpet down and sings "Chinatown, My Chinatown" in a dreamy voice that mesmerizes and hypnotizes. And before we know it, the All Stars are playing their grand finale: "When the Saints Go Marching in."

All of us crammed into this tiny space are on our feet, singing along and clapping and shouting for more.

But the concert is over. A much shorter concert than I remember, only about forty-five minutes. Oh, how we want more. As we all reluctantly shuffle out, I pause at the souvenir counter and find a CD of the Sweet Emma album I'd bought so long ago. Thrilled with my find, I buy it and slip it into my purse. I'll get to listen to all those great songs once again!

Outside, the crowds have grown. We can barely squeeze out of the building. Feeling like a canned sardine, I link a finger through one of Al's belt loops. I don't want to get separated in this pulsing mob.

Music blares from nearby clubs. The thick night air throbs with shrieks of laughter and shouts among friends. Many people carry drinks. The fragrance of incense wafts over the human swarm. I'm ready for our hotel room where we can relax and savor tonight's concert.

Luckily, we spot an empty taxi creeping along and jump in. All the windows are down and the boisterous atmosphere flows through like a river as we inch along.

When we turn onto an equally crammed street, an angry commotion flares up just ahead of us. Like stunned movie patrons, we watch as a Santa who wants to cross the street is prevented by a pickup truck that can't move. Santa starts pounding on the truck's hood, shouting and cursing. Then he throws his glass of liquid on the truck's windshield.

At that, a big linebacker-sized driver in jeans and a white T-shirt jumps out, charges Santa, and throws him to the street. Screaming and shouting fill the air as the crowd gathers close. Santa jumps up. Fists fly. Santa's on the ground again. A tall, skinny Santa's elf runs in, arms flailing like windmill blades.

I look at Al. He's laughing. All I can think about is getting out of here. I don't want the fight to make its way to us. Don't want fists or drinks flying through our windows.

"Let's get out of here!" I urge the driver.

"Yeah, yeah," he says, but there's nowhere to move.

Shouting, screaming, fists, and Santas fly. And then the wail of a siren as police arrive. Within a minute, we're able to turn out of the neighborhood and head for our hotel.

"Aw, man!" I say, relieved to be out of the fray.

"I'll bet Santa dented that truck. You know how easily those trucks dent," the taxi driver says with a chuckle.

He and Al exchange excited comments and male-bonding laughter.

"And look," the driver says checking his watch, "it's still early on a Saturday night."

SUNDAY, DEC. 13

TOURING NEW ORLEANS

We awake from a great night's sleep in our luxurious riverside room and make our way to a bountiful buffet breakfast. The spread includes fresh fruit, yogurt, oatmeal, grits, granola, pastries and chef-made omelets among other offerings. And top-notch coffee. This breakfast, like last night's hotel room, is included in our cruise price.

Following breakfast, we register at an *American Queen* embarkation desk set up just outside the dining room. We choose early seating for dinner, get our luggage tags and our identification cards (they're the size of a credit card) for onboard purchases. Each identification card also acts as our check-out/ check-in pass when we go ashore.

The registration process is pleasantly efficient.

By 9:45 a.m., Sweetheart and I have tagged our bags, set them out for pickup and delivery to the boat, and are in our tour bus seats ready for an all-day introduction to New Orleans.

As the bus pulls out, our guide, Marty, says that in 1850, New Orleans was the richest city in the nation. "The money came and stayed here," she says.

While we drive along Magazine Street, she describes it as a six-mile stretch of small-town Americana. "It's a collection of typical old New Orleans neighborhoods."

From my window, I see French bistros, barber shops, a stationery store, juice bars, restaurants, regular bars, a hot dog stand, as well as antique stores and art galleries. The National World War II Museum is on Magazine Street.

We turn onto St. Charles Avenue. Century-old live oaks line this avenue, their thick branches forming a lazy, leafy canopy overhead. Among these gorgeous trees are equally gorgeous antebellum mansions. The bus stops so we can get off and take pictures of the stunning architecture and beautiful grounds.

Marty tells us about Loyola University and Tulane University, Notre Dame Seminary and Xavier University, each a part of this vibrant city.

One of the most historic aspects of St. Charles Avenue is the St. Charles Streetcar Line. According to Marty, it's the oldest continuously operating streetcar line in the nation, providing rides to passengers since 1835. No plastic seats on these grand old cars. St. Charles Streetcar seats are made of mahogany and the cars still have brass fittings and exposed ceiling lights. I'd love to take a ride, but we don't have time to climb aboard. Sigh. Sweetheart and I will just have to come back to New Orleans sometime and catch that ride.

By late morning we're in the French Quarter, the highest place in the city. Because of its location, it was not severely damaged by Hurricane Katrina. Our bus stops here for a couple of hours so we can all explore on our own and find a place for lunch.

Now, bathed in bright daylight, the French Quarter looks far more inviting than it did last night. Founded by the French, it was ruled for forty years by the Spanish and became an official part of the United States in 1803 as part of the Louisiana Purchase.

The French Quarter, with its colorful historic buildings, wrought iron balconies, and courtyards lush with greenery and beautiful fountains, is the only intact French Colonial and Spanish settlement within the U.S. It has existed as a residential neighborhood since 1718.

Al and I are thrilled to be able to explore a little of it. We start at the French Marketplace. This open-air market began as a Native American trading post back in the 1700s. Just steps from the Mississippi, the bazaar-like structure was built in the late 1800s. Today, individual booths selling everything from T-shirts to gater-on-a-stick fast food fill the five-block market.

Booths display local produce, specialty foods and unique drinks. Al and I split a delicious organic strawberry smoothie as we mosey about. The song "Bill Bailey" fills the place, but I can't see a band anywhere. Still, the music swirls as shoppers search for the perfect souvenir.

Horse drawn carriages stand just beyond the marketplace, eager to give tourists a ride. Al and I pass them as we head deeper into this picturesque, historic neighborhood. We wander streets lined with intricate wrought iron work and colorful flags flapping from every balcony. We stroll among buildings painted in exotic pastels: greens and oranges and blues. Even now, in the brightness of mid-day, music makes its way along the streets, tip-toeing out of doorways and filling the air like a gentle fragrance.

The Quarter is a genuine melting pot reflecting cultural influences from the French, Spanish, Sicilians, Italians, Africans, Irish, and others who have called this place home. And here we are, walking its narrow streets, soaking in its spirit. We take a turn, and there kitty-corner from us stands the Pere Antoine Restaurant. The place is packed, filled with noontime conversations as waiters squeeze between tables to deliver platters of seafood. Still, the host finds us a table for two.

Hot, humid air breezes through as antique ceiling fans circle lazily above. Despite the crowd, we feel comfortably unhurried. This is our easy-does-it afternoon.

Al's order of seafood jambalaya and my blackened chicken Caesar salad are delivered to our table with a smile. The food is spectacular! The congenial babble of voices envelopes us like gentle background music. Obviously, we found a winner right here at the corner of Royal and St. Ann.

After lunch, we poke our noses in galleries, savoring the paintings and sculptures of myriad artists, while on the streets musicians' ear candy drifts easily on the afternoon air. We pause to visit with a guitarist and drop a couple of bills in his instrument case. Farther along, we also drop some coins in an accordionist's cup.

A shotgun Creole cottage calls to me, and I wish we had more time to explore. But we don't. In case you're not sure what a shotgun cottage is, it's a narrow house, usually about twelve-feet wide, with aligned front and rear doors such that a shotgun could be fired in the front door and the bullet would go out the rear.

Heading for the bus, we quicken our pace through Jackson Square. At one side of the park stands the imposing Saint Louis Cathedral with its three huge steeples. This is the oldest cathedral in the U.S. I want to go inside and see its colored windows and breathe its sacred air, but we don't have the time. Hurrying past dozens of artists and their paintings, we make it back to the bus just as the driver starts the engine.

And we're off to St. Louis Cemetery #3. This cemetery contains some of the most elaborate graves in the city as well as many beautiful statues. The above ground tombs are called *houses*. And they're shaped like houses or chapels. Built of marble or stone and topped with angels or crosses, they stand taller than Al. Many are adorned with sculptures.

Because New Orleans is below sea level, underground graves cannot be managed successfully. Guide Marty says the Spanish knew how to bury on top of the ground, and their practices continue to be used today.

St. Louis Cemetery #3, one of our stops on the tour of New Orleans.

St. Louis Cemetery #3 includes about ten thousand multiple-use burial sites, including condo-like mausoleums, wall vaults, individual family tombs, and society tombs. The artful cemetery is still in use today, but there are no funerals in progress as we tour the grounds.

The three main aisles look like grassy streets to me, lined with intricately sculpted marble houses side by side, one after the other. The sight is slightly overwhelming. These tombs hold more than one body, according to Marty, and they're used generation after generation.

As Al stays with Marty and the group, I wander around and take pictures. Clouds gather above us, lowering the temperature and causing people to remove their sunglasses. A doodling wind swirls dried leaves around the graves. Is this a welcome or a warning?

Unlike any graveyard I've ever seen, this one is a museum of fascinating architectural artworks.

The cemetery is close to our next stop, City Park. We unload at a City Park cafe named Morning Call. This is our afternoon beignet and coffee stop. Beignets are deep-fried pastries with powdered sugar coating. They're famous in this city, and I'm pleased to be able to sample one.

While I'm loving this tour, I'm beginning to grow restless. I want to get on the boat. It's well beyond two in the afternoon. I wonder how much longer we'll be touring New Orleans.

Following our beignet break, a fellow from Project Homecoming—a local nonprofit—climbs aboard and gives us an eye-opening look at the Hurricane Katrina-damaged areas, and he explains how the city's recovery effort is going.

He says that during the gigantic hurricane, eighty percent of New Orleans was under water.

"More than one hundred thousand houses were destroyed or gutted," he says. "And so far, fifty-five thousand have been rebuilt." He emphasizes that more than two thousand Project Homecoming volunteers are working to restore storm-ravaged areas.

As we drive by desolate sections of the city, and then through areas that are being rebuilt, I'm reminded of all the goodness in the world. How many people there are who care about others, who help when help is needed.

For years, I worked as a reporter on a daily newspaper in the California foothills of the Sierra Nevada Mountains. I reported on murders, car wrecks, wildfires and other tragedies. Those things made the news because they were unusual. They were not the norm.

The norm is less flashy, less garish and far quieter than attention-grabbing tragedies. The normal state of affairs is people helping people. People caring about others and about the environment. Fire fighters, first responders, teachers, doctors, volunteers of all ages and races whose response to tragedy is to help when help is needed.

This afternoon's glimpse of how New Orleans is rebuilding and restoring hurricane-damaged neighborhoods reminds me of all the goodness in the world and makes me happy.

ALL ABOARD

Our bus drops us off at the *American Queen* at three in the afternoon. This big, beautiful vessel looks like it just sailed out of the Victorian era. It's four hundred and eighteen feet long, eighty-nine feet wide. Six decks of pearly white gingerbread with a bright-red paddle wheel at the back and towering, fluted, black smoke stacks at the front.

In the steamy afternoon sunlight, *American Queen* is a sultry work of art, inviting us aboard.

Thoroughly seduced, we climb the long outside staircase leading to Deck Two. Al's knees don't do well on stairs, so we make our way slowly and carefully. At the top, we step into a genuine antebellum world. On our left is the Gentlemen's Card Room, complete with heavy wooden tables, leather chairs, even a stuffed boar's head decorating one wall. I can easily envision a nineteenth-century riverboat gambler dealing cards at one of the tables.

To our right is the Ladies' Parlor, its tall windows spilling afternoon sunlight into the elegant room filled with lace-covered chairs, Victorian artwork, even a fainting couch.

Straight ahead is the stunning Mark Twain Gallery. This is the room I'd seen online that grabbed my heart and imagination. A wide, long, mahogany-paneled room, it is resplendent in ornate period furniture and rich fabrics. There are couches, leather chairs and upholstered wingbacks. Colorful Tiffany lamps stand on hand-crafted antique tables next to every reading chair. Glass-fronted bookcases display volumes by Mark Twain and others.

Al is fascinated by a four-foot-long paddlewheeler model. It sits within a glass box on a long, wooden table in the middle of the room. "Isn't this incredible?" he exclaims, captured by the intricate detail of the decks and paddle wheel.

Not far from the ship model, a Remington baby grand piano simply begs to be played. Gorgeous Christmas trees, decked out in golden ornaments and bright lights, stand like sentinels on either side of the far doorway.

Inconspicuously tucked into a back corner is a small bank of computers, offering internet and printing functionality for passengers. This is something we've never seen on an ocean cruise. Not that I want to spend any time online when I have this floating masterpiece to enjoy, but, still, free internet on a cruise is exceptional.

Beyond the Mark Twain Gallery is the Purser's Lobby, where customer service desks are located: the Purser's desk, shore excursion desk, future cruises desk, spa appointment, and other service desks. This is also where we can find the gift shop.

There's more on this deck—the Engine Room Bar and access to the engine viewing area—but we're eager to find our room, so we'll finish our exploration of Deck Two later.

A sweeping stairway, adorned in red poinsettias and evergreen boughs, leads to Deck One. We climb plainer steps up to Deck Three, Texas Deck. At the top we find the elevators, welcome help for aging knees and hips.

Texas Deck is our deck. Our room, #374, even has a name: St. Genevieve. How cool is that? St. Genevieve, as you may know, is the patron saint of Paris.

Opening the door, we enter a little gem of a room, our home for the next eight days. Although small—about 140 square feet—it includes a queen-size bed, bedside table with telephone for onboard calls, a minimal closet, four dresser drawers, three cubbies (one with a safe) and a flat-screen TV.

Our TV and the computers in the Mark Twain Gallery are the only obvious nods to the twenty-first century on this exquisite vessel.

Laying on the bed are two old-fashioned room keys (real keys, not plastic cards), two copies of the *River Times* (the daily newsletter), a catalog of future cruise offerings, and an *American Queen* tote bag.

Antique wallpaper, historically fashionable bedside wall lamps, and artistic crown molding add style and warmth to our cabin.

The bathroom is larger than most ocean cruise ship bathrooms. Like the bedroom, it is period perfect, right down to the shower's black and white tile. A full-length mirror hangs on the back of the door, along with a hair drier. The towels and washcloths are fluffy, and it looks like the soap, shampoo, and hair conditioner are top quality. If there's anything missing, it's enough counter space to spread out our toiletries. But who's complaining? This place is a splendid little jewel! And it's ours for the cruise.

Al programs the safe while I unpack our bags, which were waiting in our room when we arrived. A pleasant surprise hangs in our tiny closet: two thick, cozy white robes. Below them sit matching slippers. Ours to use during the cruise.

When Al finishes with the safe, he wants to keep exploring. "Come on," he says, "I want to show you what's at the end of the hall."

I can tell he studied the various decks on his computer before we left. So, we head down the hall toward the boat's bow. And there, at the end of our hallway, I discover a charming eatery: the Front Porch Cafe.

All white with window-walls, glass-topped wicker tables, and lazy, overhead fans, the Front Porch Cafe has a deep Southern charm that warms me. The fragrance of fresh-baked cookies draws us in. Al finds the chocolate chip and peanut butter cookies in short order.

Our inside room and bath.

We learn that this cafe, which has about a dozen tables, serves casual fare for breakfast, lunch and dinner. And in between mealtimes, it offers popcorn, soft-serve ice cream, cookies, sandwiches and more.

Espresso, soda, and juice machines stand against one wall.

Windows look out on the boat's front porch, a huge, covered deck filled with rocking chairs and swings, tables and comfortable chairs. Obviously, if there's no free table in the cafe, you can carry your food out to the Front Porch and eat as the river flows by.

While Al scoops up a generous handful of cookies, I try to figure out the espresso machine. As I'm studying the various choices—espresso, cappuccino, different kinds of lattes—a tall, thin young man wearing an *American Queen* T-shirt approaches.

"Let me help you with that," he says. In a gentle voice, he explains and shows me how to make two lattes just the way Sweetheart and I like them. His name tag reads Jeffrey.

"Thank you, Jeffrey," I say.

He smiles. "No problem."

So nice to know right from the get-go how to make my kind of latte.

Even though Al and I are the only people in the cafe, we take our cookies and coffee out onto the inviting Front Porch and settle at a railing-side table for two.

From Mark Twain's *Life of the Mississippi* to Oscar Hammerstein's "Old Man River," the allure of this majestic waterway weaves its way through the very heart of our national culture. While Al and I enjoy our sweet repast, the afternoon sun warms the air, gulls caw loudly as they glide past, and I feel like the river is already filling up my heart.

Al's Favorite Way to Start a Cruise

As veteran ocean cruisers, Sunny and I have learned that the Realtor's maxim "location, location, location" also applies at sea. Nowhere is this truer than in a big ocean ship with thousands of passengers. With cabin deck halls resembling endless freeways, it can be a long trek from cabin to buffet or showroom. And distance counts especially for us of . . . what's the polite phrase? . . . . reduced mobility.

There's a strategy to picking your cruise cabin. Thus it was with utter delight when I first looked at the American Queen's *deck plan. There were inside cabins, our short-cruise favorite. None located a mile or more from the gangway. None adjacent to the ship's boiler-repair shop. Just pleasant inside cabins.*

Most of the inside cabins are on the American Queen's Texas Deck. And here's what thrilled me, here's what's important about the Texas Deck location: it has at the bow of the ship, the Front Porch Cafe and adjacent Front Porch. Our cabin opens onto the not-so-long hall that leads to the Front Porch Cafe. Just a gentle meander from our cozy inside cabin, a short stroll on "reduced mobility" knees.

The first thing Sunny and I do when we get on any ship is (a) drop the carry-on luggage; (b) hit the loo; and, (c) head for the buffet.

That's the crucial first event of any voyage. That first meal shows the quality of the food and demonstrates the skill of the chef. It sets the stage for the whole voyage.

When we walked into the Front Porch Cafe, aglow with late-afternoon sun and fragrant with fresh-baked cookies, I knew we'd arrived in paradise. And it gets better. Sunny found the espresso machine and made us both steaming lattes.

We took our bounty to the Front Porch proper, sitting near the bow, watching the river. Feasting.

I went back for a second round of cookies. That's when I spotted the serve-yourself soft-ice cream machine. Cup or cone, vanilla, chocolate, or both. I recommend both.

And so our voyage began. Clearly, this is going to be a first-class trip.

* * *

Following our Front Porch Cafe repast, we continue exploring. Riding the elevator up one deck, we enter the Chart Room where we find the official *American Queen*'s river-info library. This room is directly above the Front Porch Cafe.

One of the most architecturally nautical rooms on the boat, the Chart Room's large, sturdy ship's wheel dominates the space. Its polished wood gleams in front of a bank of windows. I can imagine captains of old standing at the wheel, using it to steer around snags as the paddlewheeler chugged up river. Today it's purely decorative. But there's nothing to stop you from taking hold of its handles and dreaming of commanding a steamboat all your own.

Books on the river, its history, its bird and plant life, and its towns fill two walls of bookcases. There are also novels and photography books based on the Mississippi. And true to its name, the room contains charts of various kinds relating to the boat and the river.

We walk out onto the open deck surrounding the Chart Room and feel the easy late afternoon breeze. Below this grand, open deck is the Front Porch with its rocking chairs and swings.

We ride the elevator up another level and arrive on Deck Five (the Promenade Deck). Like our deck and the Chart Room Deck, this deck is mostly filled with staterooms. But, at the rear—the stern in boat talk—stands the River Grill Bar where hamburgers and hotdogs with all the trimmings are usually available. Unfortunately, because of the December weather, the River Grill Bar is closed for the season.

An open deck surrounds the bar, and far below sits the gorgeous, red paddle wheel. We lean over the railing to get a good look at it. This twenty-eight foot wide wheel weighs twenty-three tons. Its eighteen oak paddles will help power us upriver to Memphis, Tennessee.

What I like best about this deck is the calliope. Yes, the *American Queen* has a genuine, old-fashioned, steam calliope.

Along the curved roof of the River Grill Bar stands a gleaming line of thirty-seven gold-plated brass pipes, specially built for this boat. Each sounds a different musical note when steam from the boat's engine rushes through it (think church organ pipes). A nearby keyboard operates the pipes. I can't wait to hear this calliope play. We read in our boarding documents that it plays every time the *Queen* leaves port.

We ride the elevator to Deck Six, the top deck. Here is where we find the athletic club and the pool. Like our room, the athletic club and the pool are Lilliputian. I doubt either gets much use, especially during a December cruise. The pilot house and the two black smoke stacks are also on this deck.

Due to the boat's size, the pilot house and smoke stacks retract into the superstructure if the *Queen* has to reduce its height to duck under bridges along the way.

This entire boat is wrapped with outer promenade decks adorned with architectural gingerbread. Outside metal stairways lead from deck to deck. Here on the highest deck, shaded seating areas stretch along both sides of the boat, providing peaceful areas to sit and read or watch the passing scenery. And overhead, a line of U.S. flags fly in the afternoon breeze.

Back in our room, we glance through the *River Times* and learn that there's a movie theater on our deck. Tomorrow afternoon, the holiday movie *It's A Wonderful Life* will be shown there. Hopefully, we'll be able to catch it.

At four-thirty, all passengers gather for a safety drill. Al and I are used to these kinds of drills from the ocean cruises we've taken. Just like the ocean cruise drills, every passenger is required to take part. During these gatherings, we learn how to put on our life jackets, where to go and what to do if there's an emergency.

I always feel better after these pre-cruise drills, secure in the knowledge of what to do during an emergency. Unlike our ocean cruises with thousands of passengers, this drill takes only a few minutes.

As we head back to our room, the *Queen* moves out from shore, beginning our journey up river. We can hear the calliope playing far above us. It sounds like cheerful circus music and makes me laugh.

Dinner in the J.M. White Dining Room

During our afternoon explorations, we missed Deck One. That's where the J. M. White Dining Room and the Grand Saloon are located, as well as the Captain's Bar and its nearby lobby.

The lobby and its grand piano create a spacious, comfortable area between the dining room and the Grand Saloon. An area where classic love songs from the '40s and '50s can spring from the keyboard, surrounding passengers with nostalgic memories.

While the *American Queen* doesn't have formal nights like some ocean cruises, and while it encourages casual dress throughout the trip, dinner requires wearing something more than jeans and T-shirts.

Al dons a pair of black slacks and a long-sleeved gray shirt. He even adds a tie. I wear black silk slacks and a multi-colored silk top with three-quarter sleeves. At the elevators, we encounter quite a crowd—everyone who chose five-fifteen early dining. Some couples are far more formally dressed than we are, but most match our evening attire. There's an air of excitement as we ride down to Deck One. What will dinner be like?

We're greeted with a smile and are led to a round table for eight. We're the first to be seated here. The upholstered green and gold chairs welcome us with comfort. The table, with its crisp white linen, crystal goblets and wine glasses, golden chargers, and fresh flowers, is a work of art.

The entire room can best be described as opulent. Its two-deck high arched ceiling and sophisticated globe chandeliers fill the space with a sense of serenity. Large windows on both sides, topped with stained-glass transoms, offer unobstructed river views. And the entire room is festooned with evergreen garlands.

The dining room is fashioned after a celebrated room on the historic *J.M. White* steamboat. A side-wheeler, described as a floating palace, the *J. M. White* was built in 1878 and burned in 1886. But its reputation as the most luxurious steamboat ever built has continued through the years. And this dining room maintains the stylish tradition it set so long ago.

One of the pleasures of cruising is the people you meet. More often than not, they're well-traveled with plenty of interesting stories to share. Soon we're joined by two other couples: Fred and Jeri from California, and Janet and Paul from Las Vegas. Fred and Jeri are Corvette enthusiasts. Janet and Paul are exploring America in their RV. These will be our dinner companions throughout the cruise.

After introductions, we all study our menus. The nightly five-course dinners are said to showcase America's heartland and Southern heritage. Sweetheart and I order the same thing: Blue crab and asparagus mousse for appetizers, and braised sea scallops with polenta for our entree.

We don't have the appetites we had when we were younger, so a three-course dinner will do. There's no way we can skip dessert. I get peach cobbler a la mode. For Al: lemon sorbet. Sweet endings to a perfect meal.

After dinner, we pause near the Captain's Bar to listen to Phil Westbrook play the piano and sing classic American love songs. At least a dozen other couples are also listening. Some sing along.

Then at seven-forty-five, the early-dinner crowd enters the Grand Saloon for the evening's entertainment. Another fabulous two-deck high room, the Grand Saloon resembles a small-town opera house from the nineteenth-century, with details modeled on Ford's Theater (in Washington, D.C.). An ornate lighted proscenium arch frames the stage. The place is awash in gold and red. I am totally taken with this boat, this floating work of art.

Red velvet chairs form the rows of theater seats. Above them hang enormous crystal chandeliers. Above the stage on either side, theater boxes offer slightly private views. And all around the theater hang swags of evergreen.

The Grand Saloon, where daily Riverlorian lectures and evening entertainment take place.

Tonight's program is an introduction to the *American Queen's* entertainers.

On stage, Cruise Director Alex Bernhardt welcomes us and then opens the show by singing "It's the Most Wonderful Time of the Year." The song mirrors my feelings exactly.

He then introduces Riverlorian Bobby Durham. The *Queen's* Riverlorian, he explains, is the resident history and culture expert. Bobby will present daily lectures about the Mississippi. Lectures I do not want to miss. But tonight, Bobby brings his banjo and singing voice and entertains us with "Lulu's Back in Town."

It's a funny, energetic song from the 1930s and puts us all in a playful spirit.

The boat's band, The Steamboat Syncopators, takes the stage to play several rousing New Orleans' jazz numbers. The musicians are great. Their trombone, clarinet, trumpet, drums, and piano fill the theater with such lively music that the audience joins the beat, clapping in time with the music. There's a tip of the hat to Elvis, as the pianist and guitarist play and sing "All Shook Up."

Then the four singer/dancers who comprise the *American Queen's* troupe take the stage. They are handsome, beautiful, talented, and exuberant. I know we're going to love their performances as we chug our way upriver for the next several days.

Tonight's program ends with the troupe and Alex Bernhardt singing "Old Man River." This first night's presentation gives us a taste of what we can expect for the rest of the cruise. It's going to be a lot of fun.

Before returning to our room, Al and I walk out onto the Front Porch, find a couple of rocking chairs, and enjoy the nighttime fragrance of the mighty Mississippi.

We're really here, on the greatest river in the country. I try to imagine the native peoples for whom this river provided transportation, abundant food and clean water: the Choctaw, Chickasaw, Quapaw, Osage, Caddo, Natchez and Tunica. What was life along the river like for them? Whatever the answer, it certainly changed once Europeans headed for the Americas.

In 1541, the Spanish explorer Hernando de Soto discovered the mighty waterway as he and his soldiers searched for riches he could confiscate and take back to Spain. He is assumed to be the first European to set eyes on the Mississippi. Was he impressed with the power of this great waterway? Did it fill his soul with wonder, the way it's filling mine tonight?

Ironically, one year after discovering the Mississippi, he died of a fever on its banks and was buried within its waters.

An interesting tidbit: While searching for riches in the forests of North Carolina, De Soto's expedition accidentally released pigs they'd brought along for food. Those hogs survived and became the ancestors of today's feral razorbacks found throughout the southeast U.S.

These and many other thoughts fill me as our boat paddles along.

Back in our room, I take a long shower and wash my hair. The bathroom gets very steamy and neither of us can find a fan to thin out the steam. No matter. We slip into our plush robes, recline on our comfortable bed, and click on the TV. Almost as quickly as we turn it on, we turn it off. It's been a long day. We're ready for sleep. And we don't want to break the antebellum spell surrounding us.

MONDAY, DEC. 14

NOTTOWAY PLANTATION

We awaken early after a deep and restful night's sleep. It's too early for a dining room breakfast, but last night Al requested morning coffee service, and just as I finish brushing my teeth, I hear him answering a knock on our door.

Peeking out from the bathroom, I see our stateroom attendant with a tray bearing two cups of steaming coffee, cream, and sugar. He sets the tray on our bed and wishes us a great day.

The two of us fix our drinks just the way we like them and mosey out to the Front Porch where we settle at a table to enjoy our coffee and the crisp morning Mississippi air.

A table for two on the Front Porch.

This river has been an important trade and travel route for centuries. Records reveal human habitation along its banks dating back more than five thousand years.

In the 1700s, its waters formed the primary western boundary of the young United States. From rafts and canoes to flatboats, keelboats, steamboats, and, today's barges and oil tankers, for centuries the Mississippi has throbbed with the shipping life. And here we are, sipping our morning brew, feeling privileged to be riding this great historic river in a genuine work of art.

We could have a light breakfast at the Front Porch Cafe—bagels, oatmeal, et cetera—but we choose to wait until the dining room opens at seven.

At the front of the dining room stretches a long, heavily laden buffet table. Trays of fruit and pastries, hot offerings including creamy grits, oatmeal, Andouille (sausage) hash, biscuits and gravy, scrambled eggs, and more await us. If we want to join the line at the personal omelet station, we can have a custom omelet with all the ingredients we want.

Instead, we join the buffet line, filling our plates with scrambled eggs and fruit. Once settled at a table, a waiter comes by with coffee and juice. Breakfast feels as elegant as dinner felt last night.

Today will be full. We're scheduled to land at Nottoway Plantation this afternoon, and this evening we'll attend a special Christmas Ball there. Between now and our landing, onboard activities prevail.

At eight-thirty, Sweetheart and I, along with dozens of others, make our way to the Grand Saloon for the Riverlorian lecture: "Discover the River." Al and I are determined to catch all of Bobby Durham's daily lectures. We want to learn as much as possible about the Mississippi, this grand river we've paid very little attention to.

Today, we learn that the *American Queen* is the largest steamboat ever built. Bobby emphasizes that the bright-red, wooden, steam-driven paddle wheel is not just for show. It actually supplies fifty percent of the boat's power. The rest is supplied by a set of diesel-electric propellers known as Z-drives, one on either side of the paddle wheel.

He says we'll see lots of boats as we progress upriver: towboats, oil tankers, paddlewheelers, and an array of other kinds of boats.

"And you might even see an alligator or two," he adds.

He says that on the river, down bound vessels have the right of way. "I always get questions about towboats," he says. "Towboats don't tow. They push. What they push are barges. And the barges, lashed together, are called tows. Most barges are thirty-five feet wide and about two hundred feet long.

"You'll see towboats pushing tows carrying construction materials, coal or gravel, oil, chemicals, iron ore, just about anything that's big and bulky. Covered barges are usually carrying agricultural loads like grains."

He says the average tow contains about fifteen barges and can carry as much freight as a line of semi-trucks thirty-five miles long.

He explains that steamboats don't dock like ocean cruisers. Instead they land. They put their bow in the mud and tie up. This afternoon, we'll be tying up at Nottoway Plantation.

Bobby's River Chat lecture is followed by a shore excursion orientation. Al and I stay in our seats for that. We learn that the hop-on, hop-off bus tours require maps and a boarding pass. Maps and passes can be picked up on Deck Two at the Purser's Office each day.

The boarding passes are time-specific. To keep things moving smoothly with the buses, there are only so many passes for each half hour. So if you want a pass at the same time everyone else wants a pass, you're likely to be disappointed. First come, first served.

We learn that as the buses make their route of each river town, they stop at their pick-up and drop-off points about every fifteen minutes.

The last bus gets us back to the boat half an hour before departure time.

The Shore Excursion Team discusses the various premium shore excursions. These are specialized, in-depth tours that cost extra. Al and I will skip the premium excursions. We're happy to explore the river towns along our cruise route using the hop-on, hop-off buses that come as a complimentary part of the cruise.

Following this presentation, we go to the Front Porch Cafe for a latte. Al gets a couple of cookies to go with his coffee. I notice Jeffrey helping other passengers learn to operate the espresso machine.

Then it's back to the Grand Saloon for Captain Brent Willits' Welcome Aboard. This lovely tradition includes complimentary mimosas and introductions to the members of his crew. Since we don't drink alcohol, we're given orange juice for the toasts.

Captain Willits, who looks quite stylish with his well-trimmed goatee and dress uniform, introduces the Chief Purser, the Maître D', the Guest Services Manager Alex Stylianou, and the Cruise Director, Alex Bernhardt, whom we met at last night's musical performance.

The captain gives us a little background on each crew member, welcomes us aboard, and then lifts his glass. Everyone in the Grand Saloon follows suit.

It's a brief welcome, and now we all know a little about the various people we may interact with on board. Just like last night's introduction to the performers, it makes me feel more at home here. It's a good feeling.

Lunch in the dining room. The *Queen* is expected to land early this afternoon, and we plan to go ashore as soon as possible.

Al Watches the Landing at Nottoway

Arriving in port is pretty much a non-event for ocean cruise ship passengers. This is especially true in today's world of side thrusters and Azipod engines, all of which can push a huge vessel effortlessly sideways against the dock.

Such is not the case for steam-powered paddlewheelers, however, as we learned in this morning's Riverlorian lecture. Paddlewheelers don't dock, they land, nosing their way into the sand and silt that helps form the river bank.

I couldn't wait to watch our landing at Nottoway Plantation.

If you look at a photo of the American Queen, *you'll see at least one long gangplank sticking out from the bow of the boat, suspended by a tangle of ropes and cables, and held up by an overhead jib boom. The Greek vessels called triremes had that sort of arrangement centuries ago, used for punching holes in an enemy's vessel. But the* Queen's *long gangplanks are used for letting passengers off.*

As we approached the landing at Nottoway Plantation, I joined a goodly number of other "mature" males watching from the Front Porch. We all leaned over the railing as the Queen *met the submerged sandbar with a gentle bump.*

Half a dozen crewmen in waist-high waders and waterproof vests then jumped into the cold, muddy water and began searching for tie points. The river is high, and the tie points are submerged. But the men searched with their arms and with long poles, and after much discussion and hunting, they found the ties and firmed-up the landing.

Finally, one of the red gangplanks was lowered, landing onto a wide sand and gravel path that leads up and over the river levee.

And there we were, firmly secured at our first port. I couldn't wait to explore Nottoway Plantation grounds.

* * *

Even though it's December, the afternoon sunshine warms us as we disembark, eager to check out the South's largest remaining antebellum plantation house. It's quite a walk from the boat, up and over the levee, and to the mansion. We enter the grounds through large white gates adorned with evergreen swags. The mansion is huge—three stories of white pillars and black wrought iron railings. The second and third stories are each more than fifteen feet high.

To the left of the mansion stands a Christmas market, set up specifically for the passengers of the *American Queen*. We wander over to see what goodies are available.

Cakes and candies and cookies and Christmas tree ornaments and other seasonal trinkets entice. The women running the market are all in fancy plantation dress. The feeling is cheerful. From the market, we turn and stroll around the mansion.

Completed in 1859 at a cost of eighty thousand dollars (more than two million in today's dollars), Nottoway Plantation house has 53,000 square feet of floor space. That's 10,560 square feet larger than an acre.

Built by John Randolf, a wealthy cotton and sugar farmer, the stunning house is set among beautiful grounds filled with majestic old oaks. Randolf wanted his house to be the grandest plantation house on the river. It features twenty-two massive exterior columns, twelve hand-carved Italian marble fireplaces, six interior staircases, and three modern bathrooms with running water. Among its innovations for the times were flushing toilets, gas lighting, and coal fireplaces.

Randolf and his wife, Emily, and their eleven children called this mansion home.

Their slaves, more than a hundred of them, lived in forty-two cabins, lined up in even rows behind the main house. Each cabin had two rooms and a fireplace.

The slave housing area, called The Quarters, included a communal bath house, a hospital, and a building used for childcare during the week and church on Sunday. None of the original slave cabins remain.

Al and I forgot to pick up our house tour tickets, so we won't see any of its sixty-four rooms, six interior staircases, one hundred sixty five doors and two hundred windows, nor its semi-circular white ballroom with Corinthian columns and hand-cast archways.

Isn't it amazing what you can create when you have a lot of free labor?

A side view of Nottoway Plantation House.

Since 2008, recent owners have spent more than fourteen million dollars on a complete restoration of the grand home. The place is now a resort destination complete with on-site salon and spa, tennis and basketball courts, deluxe guestrooms and corporate suite units. But the star is the plantation house, standing in all its antebellum glory.

While Al continues to wander and take pictures, I sit on a bench under one of the trees and listen to a little bird on a nearby branch sing its heart out.

Back onboard, we go to the movie room to watch *It's A Wonderful Life*. The movie room seats about fifty. A large flat screen TV at the front of the room serves as the movie screen. I recognize the young woman who is setting up the DVD. She was one of the singers in last night's program.

"Are you one of the entertainers onboard?" I ask.

She blushes and nods. Her name is Tawny Fey.

I ask how she got into show business.

"I studied sociology in college," she says, a slight Southern accent to her words, "but I wanted to sing. I'd sung in church, and I loved it. So, when I heard that the *American Queen* was holding auditions, I auditioned."

"And here you are," I say with admiration.

Cruise Director Alex Bernhardt walks up just as I'm telling Tawny how much we enjoyed last night's program. I quickly head to where Al is saving me a seat.

Alex welcomes all who have come for the movie, and points out the complimentary bags of popcorn and bottles of water on a table at one side of the room. He introduces the classic holiday film, urges us to enjoy ourselves, then he and Tawny turn out the lights and we settle in for a good time.

As always, the story moves me to tears. The message that each person's life has value far beyond what we can imagine, is never out of date. Following the film, it's nap time.

Our Holiday Ball

Al and I slip into the dressiest dinner attire we brought—a suit and tie for him, a silk outfit and golden shawl for me. And off we go to the Christmas Ball at Nottoway Plantation.

I'm really cold walking down the gangplank under black winter skies. The breeze coming off the Mississippi is sharp, and I squeeze closer to Al. Fortunately, the *Queen* arranged for golf carts to take us to the mansion. They're not antique, but they're very welcome as they carry us up and over the levee and close to the front of the mansion.

The walkways, stairways, and balconies are all alight. The entire building and grounds sparkle and glow with lights. Such beauty! We climb one of the two curving staircases to the front door and step into the twelve-foot wide, forty-foot long grand entry hall.

To our right is the White Ballroom where four men and four women in period costume are dancing to harpsichord music. The music is a waltz, but I've never seen these steps before.

A group of us from the boat stand spellbound at the doorway as the dancers glide around the room in perfect unison. The dance includes a promenade with couples touching only at their raised hands. Then, in gentle twirls, they circle and like spinning tops, choose one partner and dance in each other's arms. As the music continues, the dancers move apart and choose another partner, until every woman has danced with every man. Then the dance ends, and all dancers bow in thank you to their partners.

It's beautiful, intricate, like living poetry.

Al and I turn and make our way across the entry hall into the men's card room. This huge room is decorated lushly for the Christmas season. Under the many decorated Christmas trees are small gifts and souvenirs available for purchase. The entire place is illuminated with candle light. The glow is magical.

As we leave the mansion, Al says, "Did you notice that one of the men dancers wore a confederate general's uniform?"

I hadn't noticed. I would not know what a confederate general's uniform looked like, but I know that all the dancers wore stunning period apparel.

We now head for the Randolff Ballroom, a recent addition to the property. As we walk along the tree-lined path to the ballroom, the branches filled with tiny white lights make our way sparkle. And all along the way, costumed carolers add Christmas music to the night air.

In the ballroom, we're seated with three other couples, all from Ohio. One of the women says she and her husband have sailed on Mississippi paddlewheelers more than a dozen times.

"Every cruise is different," she says, "and we like visiting the little towns along the way."

As the first course is served—Louisiana Blue Crab Cakes with Cajun Tasso Cream Sauce—the man to my left tells me he's a farmer, specializing in corn and soybeans. He describes how his three thousand acres are planted by computers, and how all the government's environmental laws cost him dearly.

Our second course is lobster bisque. The farmer says it angers him that farmers in Brazil and China don't have to spend the kind of money and effort he has to spend in order to comply with the burden of environmental regulations.

If Al heard this conversation, he'd be amazed that I'm actually keeping my thoughts to myself as I listen to this man's experience. I'm pro-environmental regulations, believing that they preserve the best of the earth for us and for future generations. However, I can understand this businessman's financial frustrations.

My third course is pan-roasted fish topped with New Orleans BBQ shrimp. The farmer and Al both have Angus center-cut petite filet.

At this point, the farmer, who knows the other couples from Ohio, tells me about one of the men who is a retired machinist.

"He deals in farm toys," the farmer says. "There's a whole, worldwide subculture of collectors and dealers specializing in farm toys." He describes how his friend realized that the toys' original boxes were as valuable as the toys themselves, and he bought a whole bunch of them at once.

"He sold a single box for seven hundred dollars," the farmer says. And we both laugh, amazed at what people collect.

By the time we finish this main course, I'm stuffed. But we still have dessert coming, and there's no way we can turn down dessert.

After clearing our dinner plates and flatware, waiters in period attire bring each of us a generous slice of Chocolate Tuxedo Cake with chocolate mousse and ganache topping.

This bounteous dinner has been a three-hour affair, complete with lovely music, interesting tablemates and stimulating conversation. The other couples at our table excuse themselves to go to the dance floor.

Sweetheart and I wander back to the boat, feeling full and warm and happy.

The levee is topped with huge piles of wood, some as high as twenty feet tall and as we cross the levee and start down toward the river, people set the wooden piles alight. This is the traditional Christmas bonfire setting.

Most of the time, these huge riverside bonfires are set on Christmas Eve, to illuminate the way for Santa. But tonight, they've been set for those of us visiting from the *American Queen*, so we can take part in this age-old Cajun custom.

TUESDAY, DEC. 15

SAINT FRANCISVILLE, LOUISIANA

This morning's River Chat, entitled "Traveling on America's Rivers Past to Present," focuses on the many kinds of boats that have been used on the Mississippi.

This kind of lecture—interesting and connected to the cruise—is one reason we wanted to take this Mississippi River trip. We wanted to learn about a part of America we'd never paid much attention to before. Obviously, we're not alone in our desire for such knowledge, because the Grand Saloon is nearly full as Bobby takes the microphone.

He talks about Indian canoes and about French explorers and their pirogues (or dugouts). These dugouts could carry huge loads. Al and I remember reading about the

Lewis and Clark Expedition using pirogues that could carry up to eight tons. Bobby says that the most common boat for nearly two hundred years was the flat-bottom keel boat.

"It could only go with the current. So, they'd float it down to New Orleans with all the freight. Then they'd sell the goods and sell the flat boat itself because New Orleans needed lumber for homes, and they'd walk back," he says. "It was dangerous, of course, walking two or three or four months with all that cash. "Sometimes they didn't sell the keel boat, but actually pulled it upriver back to their home. That was also dangerous."

James Watt, a Scotsman, improved the efficiency of the steam engine and introduced his own steam engine in 1781. John Fitch, launched the first steamboat on the Delaware River on August, 27, 1787. Members of the Constitutional Convention observed its trial run. Robert Fulton was the first to launch a successful steamboat enterprise.

But the man who caught my interest was Henry Miller Shreve, who redesigned steamboats, making them sleeker and faster. He also added cabins so that his boats could transport passengers as well as freight, animals, and other supplies.

His steamboat, the *George Washington*, launched in 1816. It was the first steamboat with passenger cabins—eighteen on the second deck. Shreve gave each cabin a name rather than a number. He named each for one of the states in the Union. That's how we've come to call a boat's or ship's cabin a stateroom.

Shreve also created a snag boat that cleaned out the river so that other boats could safely navigate. Shreveport, Louisiana is named after him.

Following the Riverlorian presentation, Al hurries up to Deck Six to watch the boat's smoke stacks come down as we pass under the John James Audubon Bridge.

Lowering *American Queen's* Smoke Stacks

You may be familiar with the Breton Fisherman's Prayer *(I'd almost call it a lament): "Oh God, the sea is so wide, and my boat is so small." I'm pretty sure that steamboat captains have a similar version of the prayer. Theirs goes, "Oh God, the bridge is so low and my boat is so tall."*

I'd never considered this dilemma, despite my years at sea—first in the U.S. Navy, then later on our ocean cruises. Sunny and I have cruised under many bridges of great span without the slightest consideration.

Although not an ocean liner, the American Queen *is ninety-nine feet tall in full dress. That's equal to a ten-story building. A whole lot of bridges across the Mississippi aren't that far above the water, especially when the river's at full flow.*

What to do?

You'd think there are but two solutions: raise the bridge or lower the river. Right? The first isn't possible unless it's a draw bridge. And as to the second, yes, the river will lower in due time perhaps, but who knows?

However, the American Queen *has a clever third solution. Lower the boat, or at least the height thereof. The task is to lower the tallest part of the boat. This happens to be the two gorgeous, black stacks that vent engine exhaust. At forty-four feet tall and more than twelve feet in diameter each, they're big and heavy.*

I was determined to find out how the stacks were lowered as we approached the John James

Audubon Bridge near St. Francisville. I dashed as fast as my arthritic knees would carry me up the stairs to the Sun Deck to see the operation.

I envisioned something involving a cadre of deck hands, removing guy wires and other hardware. Someone on a ladder. A team with a long rope. A hairy boson's mate shouting directions. That was how we'd have done it in the Navy, though the air around the boson would be blue. [Lexicological lesson here: boson is short for boatswain, the officer in charge of the deck crew].

Nothing was like I imagined.

Instead, the stacks gracefully pivoted down, coming to gentle rest on Y-shaped cradles rising from the foredeck. That was it. No deck crew. No hairy boson. No blue air. I could almost hear Peggy Lee singing "Is That All There Is?" in the background.

As soon as we passed under the bridge, the stacks slowly rose back to their vertical position. The whole process is controlled hydraulically from manual controls in the pilot house.

But what if the boat is still too tall, even with the stacks lowered? Would we make the evening news, snagged under some bridge like a hapless semi driver caught beneath Highway I47?

Not to worry. The American Queen *has a final solution: Duck. Or, in this case, lower the pilot house. The whole thing. More hydraulics enables the pilot house to sink a full nine feet into the boat.*

The Queen *is a nimble lady who can do the limbo smooth as silk. Should you chance to voyage on the* Queen, *you mustn't miss the lowering of the stacks. Bring a video camera.*

* * *

At eleven, Sweetheart Al and I meet at the Front Porch Cafe for a hot sandwich and a latte. And at twelve-thirty, we're among the first group to board the hop-on, hop-off bus to Saint Francisville.

This quaint burg, thirty miles north of Baton Rouge, is the oldest town in the Florida parishes of Louisiana. What's called a county elsewhere is called a parish here.

Saint Francisville was once the capitol of the Republic of West Florida. Sweetheart and I had never heard of the Republic of West Florida, but, before there was a Republic of Texas or a Republic of California, there was a Republic of West Florida.

And the Republic of West Florida was a free and independent nation for all of seventy-four days. We learned about this from the hop-on, hop-off bus guide.

In the 1800s, colonials living in West Florida grew to resent Spanish rule. And on September 23, 1810, an organized group of colonists attacked Fort San Carlos in Baton Rouge, killing or wounding five Spanish soldiers and chasing off the rest. They then raised their banner—a white star on a field of blue—and declared Republic of Florida independence. Some say this was the shortest revolution in the history of our country.

The Republic of Florida, with Saint Francisville as its capitol, existed for seventy-four days until President Madison annexed it. The area is now a part of Louisiana.

Our hop-on, hop-off map shows nine points of interest where the bus will stop to let passengers off or take them on. We get off at the first stop: Royal Street.

As December's bright sun warms us, we stroll, admiring the beautiful homes and quaint shops. Although I'm not much of a shopper, I can't resist the corner brick store—Grandmother's Buttons. This unique boutique is full of fascinating button art and jewelry. There's even a button museum section where we learn some of the history of the button business.

Later, we find the site of the Republic of West Florida and remark that this trip is enriching our knowledge of American history. We briefly check out the United Methodist Church and then climb back on the bus and ride to the Museum of the West Feliciana Historical Society.

The building housing this small museum is a restored 1890s hardware store. It's a must stop for history lovers. The stories of the area are beautifully displayed in artifacts, photographs and text. From the early inhabitants, the Houma Indians, to the time John James Audubon spent here, to the "lost city" of Bayou Sara and the West Florida Rebellion, to more recent developments, this museum is chock full of fascinating information. Sweetheart and I spend at least an hour browsing.

I'm deeply moved by the story of the town's Rosedown Baptist Church. It began in the 1800s as a slave church, when the Rosedown Plantation owner gave his slaves permission to form a church of their own for weekly worship services. Following the Civil War, the church and its congregants continued.

The Museum of the West Feliciana Historical Society.

The congregation was small but faithful. The descendants of slaves worshiped every week, and when family members died, they were buried in the church's graveyard.

In 1901, the congregation—made up of African American residents, former slaves and tenants of Rosedown—moved the church to a new location on the plantation and consecrated a new building.

But in the 1990s, a developer from out of the area—some say from Atlanta, others say from Denver—bought the plantation and did not recognize the original agreement between the plantation owner and his slaves. The new owner ordered the church dismantled. He told the pastor that a church is the people, not the building, and they'd have to go worship (and bury their dead) somewhere else.

But the congregation felt the church and cemetery were sacred ground. After more than a century, the building and grounds encompassed the very personal histories of scores of local families. And its own history was a treasure none of them could give up.

Quite a fuss ensued, with newspaper articles and TV coverage. Soon the entire town of Saint Francisville joined in supporting the church and its congregation. Their combined influence forced the new owner to acknowledge and honor the original agreement. In December 1993, the church received a donation from the Saint Francisville community to buy the one acre of land on which the church and graveyard sit, thus securing its location for all time.

It's a short walk from the West Feliciana Historical Society Museum to the Grace Episcopal Church. As we stroll, we can't help but comment on the gorgeous old live oak trees draped in moss. Grace Church is a beautiful brick structure with a rose window above the door. Organized in 1827, it is the second oldest Episcopal church in Louisiana. Its organ dates back to 1860.

When we finish our exploration of the church and its surrounding cemetery, we are ready to ride the bus back to the boat. If we had the energy, we could explore other enticing places, like the Audubon State Historic Site at Oakly Plantation, or one of the other plantations in the area. But we are tuckered out, and we learned long ago to listen to our bodies and give them rest when they need it. So we ride the bus back, and head for our room and a late afternoon nap.

A Croonin' Christmas

We meet our dinner mates at our regular early seating. One indication that the *American Queen* caters to a more mature crowd is the fact that early seating reservations were the first to run out. Al and I were lucky at registration in New Orleans to get one of the last early seating reservations.

Everyone at our table tonight is talking about Saint Francisville and what they loved seeing there. Fred and Jeri rave about the Methodist Church (which we just sort of skimmed by). They especially love the 150-year-old bell.

"When it chimes, you can almost hear the history in its music," Fred says.

Janet and Paul say they borrowed *American Queen* bicycles and explored the city on wheels.

"Where are the bikes?" Al asks.

"Down on Deck One, but you have to stop by the Purser's desk and reserve one," Janet says. "There's only a few so it's first come, first served."

Paul enthusiastically describes visiting the Red Caboose, all that's left of the West Feliciana Railroad. "The railroad consisted of twenty-seven miles of track," he says, "but it was the first standard gauge and first interstate railroad system. It operated from 1828 until 1892."

The caboose now stands in the Saint Francisville Railroad Park, at the site of the original West Felician Railroad, he adds.

I share the Rosewood Baptist Church story. We all learned a lot today.

Dinner is as elegant as last night. Al has fettuccini as a starter. I get Minnesota Wild Rice Soup. It's way too salty for me, so our waitress replaces it with my own serving of fettuccini, which is delicious.

Al's entree is red snapper and shrimp Creole. I have duck breast with a tasty currant-orange sauce. Our table mates feast on steak and baked potatoes.

Al and I have crème brûlée for dessert, then hurry to the Grand Saloon for tonight's entertainment.

Every time I walk into the Grand Saloon, I'm struck by its exquisite warmth. The atmosphere is both beautiful and inviting. Tonight, the place buzzes with enthusiasm. Obviously, folks had a great time today in Saint Francisville.

When the lights dim and Cruise Director Alex Bernhardt steps on stage, all chatter stops. He asks if we had a good day and the room erupts with cheers. He talks about entertainment around the boat later tonight—at the Captain's Bar and the Engine Room Bar. He talks about tomorrow, when we'll land at Natchez, Mississippi, one of the oldest river towns in America. And then he introduces tonight's entertainment.

"And now, ladies and gentlemen, it's my privilege to introduce this evening's guest performer, an artist who has been associated with the *American Queen* since her first sailing back in 1995. Audiences love his effortless style and you will, too. So, accompanied by our own Steamboat Syncopators, put your hands together and welcome vocalist Fred Bishop."

The golden curtains part, and out steps a dashing silver-haired Fred Bishop wearing a black tux and singing "Happy Holidays." Moving gracefully across the stage and back, he radiates cheer as he segues into a jazzy rendition of "Jingle Bells" and then into an equally lively "It's Beginning to Look a Lot Like Christmas."

I can't get over how his warm baritone/tenor and these familiar songs fill me with joy. I feel that the theater's awash in musical glitter.

"Thank you," he says, accepting our applause. "It's great to be with you this week on the beautiful *American Queen*. And during this special time of the year. I hope you don't mind that I've brought along a few of my friends."

He steps behind the curtains. In a moment he's back on stage in a red cardigan, carrying a pipe, and he's clearly Bing Crosby.

"I'm dreaming of a white Christmas," he sings. A perfect Crosby impersonation. I love it.

Following Bing, he returns as his dapper self and shares a few personal facts about his singing career, his life in California, and a little about growing up in Michigan. I instantly wonder where he grew up. I spent my childhood and youth in Kalamazoo, Michigan, and wonder if he was living somewhere nearby.

His rendition of "Chestnuts Roasting on an Open Fire" sounds just like Nat King Cole: relaxed, urbane, and confident.

After visiting a little more with the audience, he excuses himself for a moment, saying he wants to bring on a couple of guest vocalists. And when he next emerges, wearing his tux and a sparkling red feather boa, I know we're in for some crazy fun.

The band plays "Baby, It's Cold Outside" and Fred alternates verses singing as Louis Armstrong and then as Carol Channing. The performance is imaginative and terrific.

I wonder how he can strain his voice to sound like Louis Armstrong without hurting his vocal chords. Likewise, the Carol Channing impersonation.

It's clear he's having as much fun as we are as he tosses the boa behind his shoulder and belts out the song with perfect Carol Channing style. The audience is so caught up in his clever performance that folks start applauding before he's even finished.

Fred Bishop is more than a crooner. He's an excellent entertainer whose versatile voice and on-stage naturalness charms us all. In a dramatic change of pace, he draws his Christmas program to a close with a lovely combination of "Ave Maria" and "Oh Holy Night."

As Al and I head for our room I'm fairly bursting with holiday spirit. And it's all because of tonight's great show.

WEDNESDAY, DEC. 16

NATCHEZ, MISSISSIPPI

We awaken to a world of fog. Like a thick, gray, dripping blanket, it covers the river, hiding banks and trees and sky.

The word is, because the river's high and flowing swiftly, we won't be landing at Natchez as early as predicted. We may only have a couple of hours to explore this city and its historic homes.

Every table is taken at the Front Porch Cafe. And there's no way we want to eat out on the Front Porch proper in this chilly-damp-gray weather. So we wander down to the dining room for breakfast, and check out the buffet line before loading up our plates.

I fill a small bowl with blueberries, strawberries, and yogurt, then help myself to scrambled eggs with mushrooms, spinach and Swiss cheese. A helping of potatoes, a glass of orange juice, and cup of coffee complete my breakfast.

Al skips the eggs, but adds two pastries.

We find an empty table for two near a window. As we take our seats, he says, "There must be two hundred dollars' worth of fresh berries at breakfast. Each day." We love fresh berries for breakfast. These alone are a gourmand's delight.

There's nothing to see out our huge tableside window. Nothing but gray. Well, we knew traveling in December meant iffy weather, so we refrain from complaining and simply enjoy our breakfast.

At nine, we go to the Grand Saloon to hear a promotional talk about future *American Queen* cruises. That's when I learn that this boat has several inside rooms designed for solo travelers. That's pretty cool.

Ocean cruise lines are just beginning to cater to solo travelers and here the *American Queen* has rooms available for people traveling alone.

All rooms onboard, from the smallest inside room to luxury suites that come with river butler service, have graceful and tasteful Victorian touches that make the cruise feel like a trip through the best of antebellum history.

This promotional talk describes in general the upper Mississippi cruises, cruises along the Ohio and Tennessee rivers, and theme cruises.

I'm interested in them all, but we don't have the money to take advantage of them. Nonetheless, I take a catalog describing all the cruises for next year. It will make for enjoyable daydreaming.

Following this presentation, we're given disembarkation instructions. I hate the idea that we're only three days into our cruise and are already getting directions on how to leave the ship when the cruise is over. I'm having too much fun to think about the end yet.

Thankfully it's a short talk. The night before disembarkation, we must have our luggage outside our cabin by eleven p.m. and we must vacate the cabin by eight the next morning.

Sweetheart bought us an airport transfer so we won't have to worry. We can have breakfast onboard and then head for the *American Queen* bus that will take us to the airport. Should be an easy departure.

After the disembarkation talk, we head for the Front Porch Cafe for a latte. While Al collects the cookies, I stand at the latte machine and push the buttons that will deliver the perfect drink for each of us.

I hear a voice behind me that I think I recognize and turn to see last night's star, Fred Bishop, waiting for his turn at the machine. He's not in a tux, but rather jeans and a blue shirt, with the sleeves rolled up. The blue of his eyes matches his shirt.

Thrilled to meet him in person, I say, "We loved your show last night. Loved the wonderful Christmas music."

He smiles. "Thank you."

I move aside with my two steaming lattes and he begins to make himself an espresso. I say, "Doesn't it hurt your throat to sing like Louis Armstrong? I'd think you'd be hoarse today."

He laughs and says, "It's a bit of a strain to sing both the Louis Armstrong and the Carol Channing voices. But I'm not hoarse today."

Now we both take our coffees and move away from the machine so those in line behind us can make their designer coffees. Al is standing by a table with a stash of cookies and waves us over. Fred and I join him.

How cool is that—sharing morning coffee and cookies with last night's star?

"I'm really curious about where you grew up," I say. "I heard you say Michigan last night. I grew up in Kalamazoo, so I'm wondering where your childhood was spent."

After a sip, he says, "The little town of Vandercook."

I've never heard of Vandercook. "Where's that?"

"Not far from Jackson," he says, breaking a chocolate chip cookie in half and popping part of it in his mouth. "Are you familiar with Jackson?"

"Sure I am. My grandmother's brother settled in Jackson."

He looks interested. "What's his name?"

"Bigalke." (Pronounced BeeGULLkey)

He jerks up straight like a bolt of lightning just struck him, and stares at me with shock. "Frank Bigalke?"

"Yes. He was my grandma's older brother." Now I'm grinning. He knows my grand uncle?

He's shaking his head like he's trying to clear it of fog. "Frank and Margaret Bigalke were best friends of our parents," he says. "My sister and I called him uncle Frank."

"That's what I called him," I say.

"Uncle Frank and Margaret were always at our house for Christmas or Thanksgiving," he adds, the sound of amazement in his voice.

I laugh at this strange but wonderful connection. "Can you believe this? We have the same uncle."

He says, "Amazing!"

"I guess that makes you two cousins," Al says.

We all laugh.Then Fred and I start sharing memories of Uncle Frank.

"He was *so* tall," Fred says.

I nod, remembering what a big man he was. "And he fought in World War I," I say. "I have photos of him in his uniform."

Fred talks about family gatherings with my uncle and aunt. I talk about Grandma and other members of our family in Kalamazoo.

When I check my watch, I see that it's time for the Riverlorian lecture. I don't want to miss it. I hate to end our family reunion, but Fred understands.

As Al and I hurry to the Grand Saloon, I say, "What are the odds of this happening at all, let alone on a paddlewheeler in the middle of the Mississippi River?"

"It's a small, small world," he says.

* * *

Today, Bobby Durham's River Chat is all about steamboats on the Mississippi. He says that during the decade of 1810, twenty steamboats worked the river. Within twenty years, more than 1,200 steamboats rode Mississippi's currents.

In those days, no one could run at night. And during the day, a steamboat could easily burn six cords of wood as it chugged along the river.

Boiler explosions were common. During the 1800s, exploding boilers destroyed five hundred vessels and killed about four thousand people. The worst maritime disaster in U.S. history is the 1865 boiler explosion and resulting fire aboard the Sultana, near Memphis. The death toll was estimated at eighteen hundred.

Bobby says the Mississippi's 2,350 miles makes it the second-longest river in North America. "When you add the lengths of its two biggest tributaries—the Missouri and Ohio rivers—the Mississippi becomes the fourth-longest river system in the world," he says, "after the Nile, the Amazon and the Yangtze."

Mississippi's watershed covers forty percent of the continental U.S., all the way from the Allegheny Mountains in the East to the Rockies in the West.

Every day when I attend these lectures, I wonder why I didn't get more information about this great river when I was in school. Then it occurs to me that maybe I did get a lot of this in school and have simply forgotten it over the years. Whatever the truth, I appreciate learning about the river and this part of the country.

Bobby says the U.S. Army Corps of Engineers maintains a nine-foot shipping channel from Baton Rouge, Louisiana, to Minneapolis, Minnesota. And a forty-five foot shipping channel south of Baton Rouge.

While I'm interested in all his information about steamboats and the river, what really grabs my attention this morning is what Bobby calls "the year of miracles." It was 1811 when a series of weird happenings in this part of the country shook people up. A twin-tailed comet, so bright it could be seen during daylight hours, lit up the sky between October and April. There was a total eclipse of the sun.

An uncommon mass migration of squirrels—tens of thousands of them, swimming across the river (and most of them drowning)—startled all who saw the brown mass moving through the water. On October 23, millions of passenger pigeons filled the sky, blotting out the sun's light.

And then there was the great earthquake of 1811. Historians who study such things estimate that the earthquake along the New Madrid fault, which runs parallel to the Mississippi River Valley, probably measured about 8.8 on the Richter scale. Towns and villages along the river were destroyed. The quake was felt as far away as Washington, D.C. Twenty-seven major aftershocks kept people in the area on edge.

Most fascinating to me is the fact that the earthquake created an eighty-mile long, seven-mile wide lake in the northwest corner of Tennessee. And the lake has remained as evidence of the great upheaval.

Today, Reelfoot Lake is a flooded forest of majestic cypress within the 25,000 acre

Reelfoot Lake State Park. The park is a major hunting and fishing preserve. The lake itself harbors numerous species of shore birds as well as ospreys and other birds of prey. In fact, during January and February, Reelfoot Lake is home to thousands of American bald eagles.

And to think, I would never have known about "the year of miracles" if I'd missed today's River Chat.

Leaving the Grand Saloon, we see that the fog is gone. But now it's raining. Thank goodness we packed umbrellas. I head for the Purser's Office to get our bus passes. A kiosk in front of the office holds all the hop-on, hop-off bus passes for the day. Each half hour slot has just enough passes to fill one bus.

Today, the first slot for noon seats is already empty. So is the twelve-thirty slot and the one o'clock slot. I can only get us passes for the one-thirty bus. That won't give us much time to explore. Oh, well, it gives us time for a leisurely lunch in the dining room.

We climb aboard the hop-on, hop-off bus at one-thirty sharp. The rain has slowed from a steady pour to something more like a heavy mist.

Our bus guide says that Natchez has been inhabited since the eighth century. It was inhabited by the Mississippian culture, the Natchez Indians, and the French before settlers began moving west.

The French settled Natchez in 1716, making the city the oldest permanent settlement on the entire Mississippi River.

Cotton—and the slave labor that planted, cultivated and harvested it—made Natchez wealthy. In 1860, it was the richest city in the U.S. Many of the antebellum mansions of those days still stand along Natchez streets.

There are nine stops on our hop-on, hop-off map. We get off at the first stop to see the Rosalie Mansion. Built in 1823 on a bluff overlooking the river, Rosalie Mansion served as General Ulysses S. Grant's Union Army headquarters during his occupation of the city in 1863.

This stunning structure inspired many Greek Revival-style mansions in the town. Today, Rosalie Mansion is owned and operated as a historic house museum by the Mississippi State Society, Daughters of the American Revolution.

It was declared a National Historic Landmark in 1989.

Back on the bus, our next stop is Saint Mary's Basilica. The only church built as a cathedral in Mississippi, Saint Mary's stands on the corner of Union and Main Streets, dominating the area. It is the oldest Catholic building still in use in Mississippi.

Its two-story brick structure with a soaring spire was originally consecrated in 1886 as a cathedral. In 1998, Rome granted St. Mary the elevated status of minor basilica. Sweetheart and I spend at least half an hour admiring the church grounds with their gorgeous old live oaks and large, ornate fountain.

The garden behind St. Mary's Cathedral in Natchez.

Then we climb the front steps and enter this architectural masterpiece. Eight huge, stained-glass windows fill each of the two main sanctuary walls. The three white marble altars were fashioned in Italy especially for Saint Mary's.

The church's spacious interior includes beautiful statuary, frescoes, plaques, and more. This serene place of worship makes a perfect stop to rest, think, pray.

After St. Mary's, we wander through portions of the downtown and are saddened by its run-down appearance. There are many empty buildings, or businesses with closed signs plastered across their windows. The area feels bleak. And the heavy gray sky adds to the feeling.

Our last stop of the day is the Museum of African American History and Culture at the corner of Main and Wall Streets. This rather plain-looking building turns out to be a treasure house packed with photos, artifacts, books, and other materials relating to slavery, Reconstruction, the Civil Rights movement, and the modern-day African American culture of the region. It holds a wealth of information on Natchez's most influential African American citizens, past and present.

We should have stopped here first. This place deserves more than a cursory visit, and we don't have enough time to do it justice.

From the stunning antebellum mansions to the African American Museum, we've gained a quick and intriguing introduction to the history of Natchez, Mississippi.

On our ride back to the boat, we plan for tomorrow's bus passes. Because we got a late start today, there wasn't enough time to really see the African American Museum. And tomorrow, we'll have only half a day in Vicksburg, so we need to get the earliest possible bus passes. At the end of today's River Chat, we learned that tomorrow's bus passes will be available at the kiosk around five today.

"I'm going to be there at five," I say. "If we can't get on the first bus, we won't have enough time tomorrow to see what we want."

Tomorrow is Vicksburg, where a significant Civil War battle was fought and Al has looked forward to visiting the town ever since we booked this cruise. So back on the boat, we freshen up, and then I go to the

Purser's Office, while Sweetheart tries to grab a little nap.

The kiosk slots do not yet hold tomorrow's bus passes. To kill a few minutes while I wait for the passes, I wander over to the gift shop—the *American Queen* Emporium. There I find the usual T-shirts and hats and trinkets, but what really impresses me is the shop's book display. There are a number of books on the Mississippi River, the Civil War, and various river towns. And there's a children's area with books, toys, and games. I'm sure this area is for grandparents, since there's really no provision on board for little kids.

Glancing out the door, I see three women at the kiosk and I hurry over to join them. Evidently, the bus passes were put in the kiosk slots while I was at the gift shop.

One of the women is busily grabbing all the eight-thirty bus passes. She's actually cleaning out the entire time slot.

"Excuse me," I say. "My husband and I want to be on the eight-thirty bus tomorrow, and I'm sure there are others who want to get on that early bus."

"I'm with a church group," she says, "and we all want to be together."

I glare at her, surprised at her brazen selfishness. That's what I consider it. I'm sure she thinks she's being helpful to others in her group.

"Well," I say, "I need two of those passes. My husband and I need to be on the first bus tomorrow."

The woman clasps her handful of passes to her chest, determined to keep them all. But one of the other women says, "Give her two. Not everyone in our group will be ready that early."

Reluctantly, the woman with all the eight-thirty bus passes counts out two and hands them to me. I hurry back to our room so we won't be late for dinner.

Our dinner tonight—wild salmon and asparagus, followed by tasty mud pie—is accompanied by great conversation. Two new women join our table: Jewels from Australia and Jennifer from Wisconsin. Each is traveling solo and loving the journey as much as the rest of us.

We all talk about what we saw in Natchez today. I share my story about the woman who hogged all tomorrow's eight-thirty bus passes. Everyone at our table is duly outraged and their outrage makes me happy. It matches my own.

Dinner is followed by a fabulous Grand Saloon show. The Steamboat Syncopators and the *American Queen* Ensemble present Bourbon to Beale, a tribute to the music, the people, and the spirit of the river. Songs celebrating Nashville and Memphis. The boat's four young performers are so talented. They can sing. They can dance. They make my spirits soar.

After the show, Al and I wander out onto the Front Porch. The crisp night air makes us squeeze close to keep warm. The black sky and the rippling black river seem to embrace us, while this whole riverboat world feels exciting and inviting. Such a lovely ending to the day.

On the way back to our room, Al grabs a cookie.

One of the outer decks at eventide.

THURSDAY, DEC. 17

VICKSBURG, MISSISSIPPI

Vicksburg's Old Court House Museum.

A quick Front Porch Cafe breakfast of scrambled eggs and potatoes. And we're on the bus at eight-thirty, riding up the hill to Vicksburg. The day is clear and cold. I'm glad we brought winter jackets for this trip. Today we need them. I'm just grateful it's not raining.

As the bus (filled, I presume, with a church group and us) climbs toward the town center, our onboard guide fills us in on the area—the conflicts between its first French colonial settlers and the Natchez Indians; how the Spanish set up a military outpost on the bluffs in 1790; and how the Americans took possession of the area eight years later.

In 1825, a Methodist minister, Newit Vick, founded Vicksburg, naming the sprawling community after himself. This city, for Civil War buffs, is best known for the brutal forty-seven-day siege that ended with surrender to General Ulysses S. Grant.

Grant's victory put an end to Confederate control of the Mississippi. The fall of Vicksburg on July 4, 1863—one day after the end of Gettysburg's battle—marked a major turning point in the war and foretold the Union's ultimate success.

As our guide talks, I'm keeping my eyes on a huge and stunning stone building. The Old

Warren County Court House, which served as a target for Union troops during the siege, is the most important historic structure in Vicksburg. Built on one of the highest hills in the city, it's the first stop on our morning exploration. This is where Jefferson Davis learned he'd been elected president of the Confederate States of America.

Cannons flank the broad stone stairway leading up to the Old Court House. We climb slowly in the bright sunshine and cold morning wind. I'm thinking of the highly skilled artisan slaves who made the bricks and built the striking Greek Revivalist structure. The more than fifteen thousand square foot building was completed in 1860.

Four porticos supported by thirty-foot Iconic columns flank the Old Court House entrances. The octagonal bell tower topped with a covered cupola made a perfect target for Union troops. And yet, the building survived the war. Today, it is Vicksburg's crown jewel and has been a museum since 1948. It was named a national historic landmark in 1968.

Inside, nine rooms are stuffed with portraits, furniture, china, silver, toys, tools, and a large collection of Civil War memorabilia. In the gift shop, you can actually buy authentic Civil War relics (such as bits of bullets), as well as typical museum souvenirs. Civil War flags adorn the walls and display cases overflow with shells and bullets from the Vicksburg battlefield. There's even a display of the different types of cannon shells used in the nineteenth century.

In the Pioneer Room, we see pre-Columbian artifacts including arrow heads, beads, Indian game pieces, pipes, and fish hooks. In the Costume Room, we see ladies' wardrobes. The Vicksburg Room displays swords, guns, and Civil War uniforms. The various war-related items fascinate Al. I find them saddening, and wander elsewhere.

When I discover an aisle thick with Civil War–era photographs, I'm intrigued. I stare at boys and men in Confederate uniforms, their faces determined or proud. I wonder how many made it home at war's end. I think about their mothers, wives, children, and how the war changed them all forever. I also think about the boys and men in Union uniforms that these photographed soldiers may have killed or maimed. And their families who were also changed forever.

While I know that nations wage war for reasons deemed vital and just, I am no fan of war. My favorite poem by Edna St. Vincent Millet exquisitely expresses my feelings about war. It's entitled "Conscientious Objector." You may want to read it sometime.

As I wander among the photographs, I find several portraying Confederate soldiers with their slaves. I'm captivated by a large portrait of a seated Confederate officer and, standing beside him, a black man whose blank face stares stoically. The officer has a rifle. The black man has none. Neither man is smiling, but there is an obvious difference in their expressions. The officer looks confident or proud. The black man's eyes are empty, staring straight ahead but not really focusing on anything.

Beneath this photograph is an index card with typewriting on it. I bend down to read the text, and it says something about how faithful the slave in the picture was to his kind, white master. The text goes on to describe how the faithful slave fully supported the Confederate cause.

"What a crock!" I think. "Just look at his expressionless face, his empty eyes. They say everything about his powerlessness. I'm sure he didn't support remaining property that his master could sell."

I'm surprised that no one has changed the text to reflect a more realistic, more sensitive understanding of the two people in the photograph. The index card with its typewritten text upsets me, and I have to leave the room.

I head up the long stairway to the second floor, where the historic courtroom is set up exactly as it was when trials were held here back in the 1800s. The large room with its jury box and cast-iron judge's dais is decorated with red ribbons and bows. Beside the judge's dais stands a Christmas tree. Even with the Christmas decorations, this room's power and authority is palpable.

Eventually, Sweetheart and I catch the bus. Our onboard guide describes two firsts that I find pretty interesting. She says the practice of selling shoes by the pair in boxes began in Vicksburg in 1884. Before that, shoes were not differentiated for right or left feet: a shoe was just a shoe. But Phil Gilbert's Shoe Parlor on Washington Street started the practice of boxing pairs of shoes, with a right and left shoe designed to comfortably fit the designated foot. A practice that today is universal.

The other first concerns the popular American beverage Coca-Cola. Although an Atlanta, Georgia pharmacist created Coca-Cola, it was first bottled in Vicksburg. Until Joseph A. Biedenharn came along, the popular drink was only sold at soda fountains. But in 1894, Mr. Biedenharn started bottling it, thus making it available to a greatly expanded market.

What once was his bottling plant has become the Biedenharn Coca-Cola Museum in Vicksburg. It's a stop on our map. One that we won't be able to visit. Instead, we stop at the Church of the Holy Trinity. This Romanesque Revival beauty was built in 1870. It's an Episcopal church, beautiful inside and out. And it's on the U.S. Register of Historic Places.

The church is huge, with thirty-four stunning stained-glass windows. Six of the windows were created by Tiffany Studios and they are spectacular. The depth of color and the way the artists were able to create a three-dimensional effect are remarkable. We linger a long time in this awe-inspiring place of worship. Its beauty helps clear out the disturbing feelings the Civil War photo of the officer and his slave stirred within me.

I find it remarkable—and confusing—that the same society at the same time can produce both deeply beautiful works of art that inspire and repugnant social structures that debase.

For our last stop of the day, we get off the bus at the Old Depot Museum situated down the hill and not far from where our boat is moored. By now, the sun is warmer and I unzip my jacket as we walk inside this attractive old building. Because of the name, and the railroad tracks running next to the museum, I expect to see railroad exhibits. There are three separate glassed-off areas with model trains. But there are also large displays of military and maritime history—model ships of all sorts including paddle wheelers, towboats, Union and Confederate gunboats.

The major display is a two hundred fifty square foot diorama illustrating the siege of Vicksburg. The diorama celebrates the failed second attack by Grant's forces. More than two thousand miniature soldiers and other figures fill the scene. The artistic work that has gone into this diorama is more than impressive. I'm just intrigued that it celebrates a failure by Grant's forces, when, in the end, he prevailed.

Al is fascinated by all that's in here, but I've had enough of Southern history and culture for the moment, so I go outside to sit in the sun until he's finished and joins me. Together we wait for the bus.

"I never expected that this little trip would be such a learning experience," he says.

I nod, "And we've been able to do it at our own pace. That's what I like."

The bus drops us near the boat, and we walk down the sloping sidewalk until we reach flat ground beside the river. That's when we notice for the first time the towering cement wall marking off the water levels for various floods. The highest flood line is for the Great Mississippi flood of 1927. That was the most destructive river flood in United States history. Its waters covered 27,000 square miles up to a depth of thirty feet, altering landscapes, ruining lives and changing the course of history.

Not far from the flood marks wall is a long stretch of riverfront murals, illustrating historic moments and picturesque scenes of Vicksburg. We don't have the time to spend on them that they deserve, but I recommend you check them out if you're ever in Vicksburg.

There was so much more to Vicksburg than we were able to see on our stop there, including the National Military Park and Cemetery and the Biedenharn Coca-Cola Museum. We'll just have to come back for another visit.

Everyone out sightseeing today must be on board by twelve-thirty. As the boat pulls away from shore, we can hear the lively calliope concert.

Family Reunion at Front Porch Cafe

Al and I find a Front Porch Cafe table and settle in with our salads and sandwiches. After our chilly visit to Vicksburg, it's great to enjoy lunch in a warm and welcoming place. Glancing around, I see Fred Bishop heading our way. He pulls up a chair of his own.

"I told my sister about our conversation yesterday and she sent me some photos to check out with you," he says, handing me his phone.

There, on its screen, is a photograph of my Uncle Frank and Aunt Margaret sitting on a couch with a Christmas tree in the background. And another of them at a holiday table loaded with a traditional Thanksgiving feast.

"That's my uncle Frank," I say. "Haven't seen a photo of him in decades, but that's him."

It's clear that Fred is still stunned by our unusual connection. To be truthful, so am I.

"My sister and I think our connection was through Margaret," he says, then adds, "This is just such a hoot!"

He goes over to the latte machine and comes back with a steaming cup. I notice that Jeffrey cleans the machine after Fred's use, and then assists an elderly woman in making her cappuccino. I ask Fred how long he's been singing on the *American Queen*.

"Since 1995," he says. "I was on the inaugural shakedown cruise from New Orleans to Pittsburgh. On that cruise, we got stuck on a sandbar for three days." He laughs at the memory. "CNN came out and covered that."

Fred says he doesn't perform on the *Queen* every year, but is always happy when he's invited back. He says his favorite songs are from the forties and fifties. "That era had so much great music, so many great voices:

Sinatra, Bennett, Crosby, Nat King Cole. It was the music I grew up listening to."

I ask what he likes about performing on the *American Queen*.

"I love the intimacy of the Grand Saloon," he says. "I've performed in very large venues and even though I liked that, I prefer the smaller, more personal venues. I like seeing the faces of the people I'm singing to. Knowing that I'm connecting with them is a real rush."

I tell him that some of our relatives are also in show business. My brother has written award-winning songs, and is a well-respected magician who has worked at Hollywood's Magic Castle. We have a cousin who worked for years as an operatic soprano in New York City.

"So maybe musical talent runs in the family," I say. "But, believe me, I'm not blessed with any."

The Sultana Tragedy

Riverlorian Bobby Durham has a long, sad story to share at today's River Chat. It's all about the Steamboat Sultana tragedy. It happened in April 1865, a month filled with triumph and tragedy.

General Robert E. Lee had surrendered in Appomattox, Virginia, on the ninth. By the fourteenth, Union Prisoners of War (POW) were being released from Cahaba and Andersonville prisons and were marching toward Vicksburg. On the evening of the fourteenth, during a play at Ford's Theater, President Lincoln was assassinated. He died two days later.

On the twenty-sixth, his assassin, John Wilkes Booth was caught and killed. That same day, Confederate General Joseph Johnson surrendered the last large Confederate army. And the Civil War was over. Union POWs, gaunt, worn-out, hurting, gathered in tents at Vicksburg, waiting for a boat ride home.

Reports from those days say when the soldiers approached the Mississippi at Vicksburg, they shouted and sang with joy. After all the misery of the war and imprisonment, they were finally going home.

The army was paying boat captains five dollars a soldier and ten dollars for each officer taken aboard.

The *Sultana*, a side-wheeler built to carry three hundred seventy-six passengers, had a boiler leak and stopped in Natchez for repairs. But when Captain J. Cass Mason learned that hundreds of Union soldiers eager for transportation north were gathered at Vicksburg, he didn't want to take the time to properly remove and repair the boiler (one of four on the boat). A proper repair could take days, and in that time, other Mississippi steamboats would load up the lucrative human cargo. So he had the bulging boiler temporarily patched and headed to Vicksburg.

There, he assured army officers that the *Sultana* could carry all the soldiers they could load aboard. And so more than 2,000 homesick soldiers squeezed aboard the boat, which already had a full complement of cargo and one hundred head of assorted livestock, as well as a few families who had bought cabins for the trip to Cairo, Illinois.

The top deck, second deck, and main deck were so crowded that soldiers could find no place to stretch out and sleep. Instead the weary, wounded, sickly soldiers, many of them teenagers, huddled together in every square foot of space onboard.

The Mississippi was at flood stage as the *Sultana* chugged upriver on April 24. By the time the *Sultana* arrived in Memphis two days later, the swollen river was about four miles wide. The crew unloaded sugar and took on a load of coal. The next stop would be Cairo, where everyone planned to get off.

But ten miles upstream, at two a.m. on the twenty-seventh, the patched boiler exploded, then two more boilers exploded in a volcanic blast heard for miles. The searing steam from the boilers turned shattered wood and broken metal into shrapnel. The boat's smoke stacks collapsed, spreading a raging fire.

Those not killed immediately by the explosion, the scorching steam, and the ferocious fire, were crushed in the panic or drowned in the frigid waters of the swollen Mississippi. Within half an hour the entire structure was aflame and the river teeming with bodies. Those who clung to logs or floating debris prayed for deliverance.

About an hour after the blast, the *Bostona II*, on its maiden voyage, came upon the still-burning disaster. Its crew pulled about one hundred fifty people from the river.

In the morning, Memphis residents awoke to a smoldering wreck caught among some trees on a bar, and hundreds of bodies floating in the water or snagged along the river's banks. About seven hundred victims made it to a Memphis hospital, but of those, two hundred died from their injuries.

It's estimated that nearly 1,800 people died in this, the worst maritime disaster in American history. Despite the magnitude of the disaster, it merited modest press coverage. The nation was celebrating the end of the war.

Lincoln's funeral train and John Wilkes Booth's death captured front page coverage.

Today's River Chat is sobering, to say the least. What a horrible ending for soldiers who thought they were finally going to get back home.

Dixieland Music

At four-fifteen, we make our way to the Main Lounge on Deck One to enjoy a Steamboat Syncopators' Dixieland concert. The drummer, bass player, banjo player, trombone player, sax, and clarinet players all stand around the piano and play their hearts out.

From "Sweet Georgia Brown," "Bourbon Street," and "Lawdy I Love the South," to

"Dinah," and "Take Me Out to the Ball Game," the music grabs us all.

The crowd grows. Every seat in the lounge is taken and people stand two deep along the walls. Some sing along with the music. A couple dances to the song "All of Me," and then another joins them. Behind the musicians, huge windows reveal the trees on the banks flowing by. As the concert continues, the sun sets the treetops ablaze. And then the evening light begins to fade.

* * *

Dinner, as always, is both delicious and fun. I enjoy oysters Rockefeller and pumpkin soup. Al has catfish with rice, black-eyed peas and greens. Dinner conversation includes train travel stories, earthquake stories, and tornado stories. And we all share the fact that, until this cruise, none of us had ever heard about the *Sultana* tragedy.

The Juggernaut Jug Band

Following dinner, it's off to the Grand Saloon for the evening's entertainment—a band from Louisville called The Juggernaut

Jug Band. From the moment the five men, all wearing hats of different kinds, take the stage, it's obvious this is going to be fun. Their instruments are an eclectic assortment from traditional guitars, a bass and harmonica, to cow bells, a washboard, a nose flute, spoons, duck calls, a kazoo, and percussion instruments I can't even begin to name.

"We play good-time, old-time music," the band's leader says and off they go, filling the auditorium with exuberance. Their songs are a rambunctious mix of jazz, blues, ragtime and swing blended in with lots of humor. The "jug" part of the name comes from stoneware crockery jugs, that the musicians blow into to add to their strange musical concoction.

Following the concert, Al goes to The Captain's Bar Lounge to listen to country western music. I return to our cabin, ready to unwind after a long, full day. Each evening, we've found chocolates on our pillows. Tonight, red and white candy canes have been left for us. How sweet.

FRIDAY, DEC. 18

GREENVILLE, MISSISSIPPI

Parked at Greenville, our last port of call on the cruise.

The boat is running late today because the river is high and fast and we're going against the current. Walking along the outside railing of the Texas Deck, I'm surprised to see the sparkling blue water rushing past. When did the river change from muddy brown to this enthusiastic blue?

After so many miles of liquid brown, it's delightful to see the lines and curls of clear blue rushing past our boat. I know that there are three hundred sixty species of fish in the river and more than a hundred species of amphibians and wonder if I'll be able to see any in this sparkling water.

We've heard that water skiing began on the Mississippi, and now I believe it's possible. When we were in the more industrial part, I couldn't imagine it, but now I can picture someone on water skis sailing along this beautiful waterway.

Sweetheart and I take a leisurely dining room breakfast. And as soon as the boat docks, Al's off exploring the town. Greenville is the county seat of Washington County, located in the area of historic cotton plantations and culture known as the Mississippi Delta.

I stay on board to join a tour of the pilot's house. I wander around the boat, visit with other passengers in the Front Porch Cafe, and wander out on deck to watch the river.

There's something so peaceful about moving water, its ripples catching the glistening sun. The light on the water is almost like sparkling tinsel for the Christmas tree. Streamers of tinsel flowing downstream. Hypnotic.

This morning's air is bracing. A cold breeze sets the rocking chairs on deck to rocking and makes me zip up my jacket. A long line of cormorants stretches gracefully across the sky. Millions of birds—songbirds, wading birds, raptors and other species—fly along the Mississippi River corridor throughout the year. Sometimes you can even see bald eagles in the tallest trees.

I wander up into the Chart Room with its large pilot's wheel, and look more closely at the bookcases lining its walls. The shelves hold volumes on the river, the delta, Mississippi river towns, and books about the Civil War. I also see *Life on the Mississippi* by Mark Twain and *A Rising Tide* by John Barry and more such literary tomes. Other shelves hold large, bound paper maps.

In the middle of the room stands a round table where you can sit and read, or study the maps. It's a small, handsome room filled with light.

The Chart Room.

I wait here until Riverlorian Bobby Durham and five others who want to tour the Pilot House arrive. Then we all set out, following Bobby. We climb the outside stairs up one deck as the cold wind grabs at our hair and coats.

And when we reach the Pilot House, we crowd inside, eager to get out of the chill wind. I'm not sure of the size of the Pilot House, perhaps twelve by twenty feet. Something like that. With all six of us and Bobby inside, it's good and crowded.

The sun pouring through the big windows belies the cold wind outside. A wide desk-type counter fills three walls of the room. It's covered with all kinds of electronic and digital equipment. Bobby describes some of the instruments: the fog horn timer, the emergency PA, two radar screens, the rudder controls, and the controls for raising and lowering the stacks or the pilot house.

He tells us that on the river, down-bound vessels always have the right of way. He shows us the depth gauge. Its computer-type screen reveals that the river depth is 10.8 feet here, where we're sitting.

"This is in addition to our eight-and-a-half-foot draw (meaning the water the boat displaces)," he says. "So this spot is really more than eighteen feet deep. Our landing is a controlled grounding," he adds. "We just kind of snuggled into the mud."

He says the boat only makes about six miles an hour going upstream. But coming downstream it can average fourteen miles an hour. He reminds us that the paddle wheel supplies fifty percent of the boat's thrust. The other fifty percent is supplied by two Z-drives, each five feet across. If something gets caught in the paddle wheel such as trash or fallen branches, the crew uses the Z-drive thrusters to spin the boat so that the river's current will wash out the debris.

He says that the stuffed pig's head on the wall in the Gentlemen's Card Room is what's left of a feral boar that got caught in the wheel and drowned.

He shows us the telegraph between the pilot house and the engine room. Using it, the pilot can tell the engine room to bring the boat to a slow stop, a dead stop, or any other thing that is needed.

Since 9/11, Homeland Security has required each boat on the river have a transponder. "This shows who is on the river, their name, speed, direction and so on," Bobby says. "This way the Coast Guard can keep an eye on everyone who's on the river."

He says each commercial transponder also keeps tabs on other boats on the river. "We communicate with others three to four miles out, so we can adjust for passing and so on," he says. Then adds, "Most of the pilots are tugboat and towboat pilots, so they know everyone else who's working on the river."

He says the *American Queen* has four pilots. Two are on duty at a time. They work twelve-hour shifts. One of the men in our group asks about autopilot.

"There's no autopilot for boats on the river," Bobby says. "The river changes constantly and an autopilot wouldn't be able to account for new bends, changing sandbars, new traffic, or anything."

I ask if the pilots rely exclusively on GPS systems.

"All pilots have and use paper maps," he replies.

He then draws our attention to a cord hanging from the ceiling. He says it's for a gold-plated brass whistle on top of the pilot house. Like the calliope, this whistle is operated by steam. A pull of the chord emits a blast of the steam whistle. The steam comes out in great white clouds. I just love the fact that I'm riding a steam-powered paddlewheeler on America's greatest river.

When the Pilot House tour ends, I head down to Deck Two. As I pass the Ladies' Parlor, I notice three people putting together a jigsaw puzzle. Another woman is at home in one of the cozy chairs where she's reading her tablet. It's clear they've all made the *American Queen* their personal abode. I also feel that this beautiful steamboat belongs to me, at least for this cruise.

Walking through the Mark Twain Gallery, I decide to stop in at the gift shop. It's empty except for the woman behind the counter. She and I strike up a conversation. Her name is Pat Taylor. She's worked on boats for twelve years, and says she loves it.

"It's wonderful meeting guests from all over the world," she says. "And river people are wonderful. Working on a boat like this is all about the heart of America."

Pat grew up in rural Tennessee. As a kid, she heard the calliope and thought there was nothing to compare to it. She says work days on the *American Queen*, while rewarding, are long. "And we work seven days a week. But this job allows me to interact with entertainers and with fascinating people from all over," she says.

"For example, one afternoon a woman came in and bought several items for gifts—jewelry, books, that sort of thing—and when she signed for them, I saw her name was Sarah Brady. I said, 'That's a familiar name.' She was the woman whose husband was wounded when Hinckley tried to assassinate President Reagan. She's campaigned for gun control ever since."

Pat says she and Sarah were able to visit for a few minutes about the importance of Sarah's work. "It's just totally impressive what she has done and continues to work for," Pat says.

Visiting the Engine Room

After my conversation with Pat, I decide to check out the Engine Room. This is more of an Al-interest thing, but I have a few minutes before lunch, so why not see what it's all about?

The stairway down to the Engine Room can be found in the Engine Room Bar at the back of the boat. The bar itself is beautiful. All polished wood, with windows looking out on the red paddle wheel as it turns behind the ship.

The white metal stairway down to the Engine Room is narrow. At the bottom is a space where you can stand and watch the engines working. The room is way too hot for comfort. The guys running the place are shiny with sweat. And I know if I don't get out of here pretty soon, I'll be shiny with sweat, too. So I head back up the stairs and to the dining room where I'm supposed to meet Al.

Lunch in the Dining Room

Sweetheart is back by noon. While we take our time with lunch, I tell him about the Pilot House Tour, and he tells me about what he saw in Greenville.

What most impressed him was the E.E. Bass Cultural Arts Center, home to the Armitage Herschell Carousel.

"Did you ride the carousel?" I ask, picturing him going up and down on a wooden horse as lively music plays.

"I wanted to, but it only operates on Saturdays," he says, eyes twinkling. "It's been spinning around for more than a hundred years, you know. So, I guess it needs to rest most of the week. But I got some very good pictures of the horses. There are twenty-four of them, and four chariots. All hand-carved and meticulously painted."

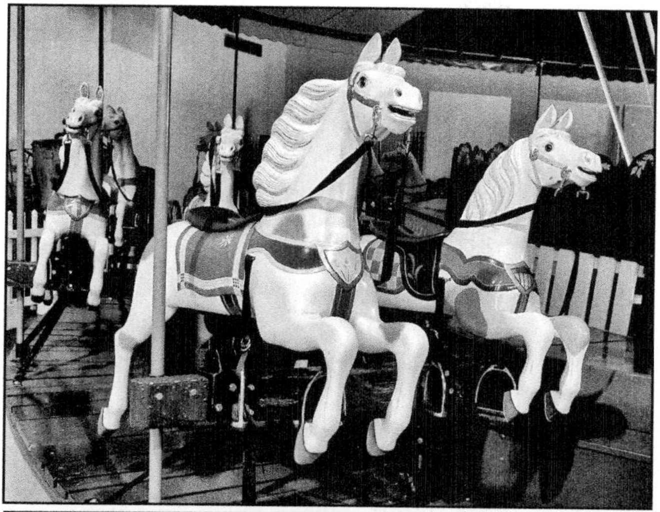

Horses on the Armitage Herschell Carousel in Greenville, Mississippi.

Two details that especially impressed Al were the real horse hair tails on the horses, and the original steam engine used to power the carousel.

"The engine isn't running the carousel today, but it's on display in the museum and it's fascinating," he says.

Sweetheart also checked out the Hebrew Union Temple, a museum on Hebrew history that was built in 1906. He didn't have time to tour the Greenville History Museum, the Flood of 1927 Museum or the Washington County Courthouse. There's also a casino in Greenville, just a short walk from where the *American Queen* parks.

The dining room bustles as we eat and share stories of our morning. Seems like everyone aboard wants to have lunch here today.

"I learned from the onboard bus guide that there are many celebrities from Mississippi," Al says. "Guess a few."

"Well, I know Elvis Presley is from Tupelo," I say. "But that's all I know about."

So Al starts naming what he can remember from the bus guide: Jimmy Buffett, Bo Diddley, Brett Favre, Jim Henson, Conway Twitty,

Tennessee Williams and Oprah Winfrey. He assures me there are many more, but he simply can't remember their names.

Although his morning in town was short, this afternoon is filled with activities we plan to enjoy. Following lunch, we make our way to Deck Five for the final calliope concert of this cruise. Since this is our last port departure until we reach Memphis and disembark, this will be our last chance to hear the ear-piercing "Beer Barrel Polka."

As the crew prepares our boat to leave, we join scores of other passengers, eager to listen one last time. The sun is bright, but the air is cold. Every River Grill Bar table is taken, and many folks are standing at the rail, waiting for the calliope concert to begin.

All thirty-seven gold-plated brass pipes (especially built for the *American Queen*) gleam in the sun. Beneath them, under the River Grill Bar roof, sits the red-and-white calliope keyboard. It's much smaller than a piano keyboard. Looks almost like a child's instrument.

But Phil Westbrook, the silver-haired pianist who performs nightly at the Main Deck Lounge near the Captain's Bar, sits on a little stool and begins to play. The musical whistles are so loud we have to plug our ears. But the music is rollicking and fun and everyone's smiling.

When Phil finishes his concert and the boat is gliding along on the water leaving Greenville behind, he announces that anyone who wants to play five or more notes on the calliope will receive a Vox Calliopus certificate. Al and I quickly get in line to play this historic musical instrument.

Most people ahead of us simply hit five random notes. But I play "Chopsticks." And Al plays a good portion of "Let Me Call You Sweetheart." "This is just a blast!" he says as his fingers dance across the keys and the bursts of white steam overhead blast out the song. When he finishes, the people around us applaud.

Chatting with a couple of regulars

Following Bobby Durham's afternoon River Chat, I get to talking with Betsy and Skip from Jackson, Ohio. The three of us are sitting in the Mark Twain Gallery enjoying the elegant beauty of the room and the wind-whipped scenery floating by outside. This is their fourteenth cruise on the *American Queen.*

"My favorite movie is *Show Boat,*" Betsy explains. "We live near the Ohio River and one day we saw the *Queen* docked and we asked for a tour, and they gave us one. I told Skip, 'This is my dream.'"

Skip says their first trip was with a tour group. "After that, she fell in love with the boat," he says with a chuckle.

I can certainly understand that. I've been in love with it since we first stepped aboard.

Skip is retired from Goodyear Tire, where he worked as a safety and training manager. He appears to be a calm, nothing-ruffles-his-feathers kind of guy.

Betsy, who was a homemaker, studied food and nutrition at the University of Akron. "I appreciate the food and its presentation here," she says.

They say they try to take a cruise a year. Sometimes it's an ocean cruise. "We've been to Alaska on Holland America, and we've cruised on the *Queen Mary,*" Skip says. "That *Queen Mary* was the worst cruise ever."

Betsy nods, but they don't offer any specifics on that disappointing trip.

I ask what keeps them coming back to the *American Queen* and the Mississippi.

"Our first *American Queen* cruise was from Memphis to New Orleans in February. We went from winter to spring," Skip says with a smile. "We liked it so much we wanted to stay on board and just turn around and go back to Memphis, but the boat back was full. I think it's the staff and the people we meet that keeps us coming back."

Betsy says, "And we love the Southern hospitality. You don't find that in other places." She pauses and then adds, "The first time you cruise on the *American Queen*, they say, 'Welcome.' The second time, they say, 'Welcome back.' The third time they say, 'Welcome back home.' That epitomizes the feeling here."

Skip adds, "On these boats you get to see how large and beautiful the U.S. is. We're amazed at the vastness of our country. Oh, and we also learned about calliopes." He chuckles. "We've both gotten certificates for playing the calliope."

I laugh, too. "Al and I are going to get our certificates. We just played it this afternoon."

Onboard Entertainment

Today's movie is *White Christmas* starring Bing Crosby, Danny Kaye, and Rosemary Clooney.

And this afternoon in the Grand Saloon there's a *Name That Holiday Tune* contest. The *American Queen* Ensemble and the Steamboat Syncopators challenge passengers' musical knowledge of holiday songs. Although Al and I opt for an afternoon nap instead, I can imagine how much fun this musical event will be for those who attend.

After a lobster dinner in the dining room, we head for the Grand Saloon to enjoy *Bravo! Broadway*. Tonight's show features the talented *American Queen* Ensemble performing songs from *West Side Story*, *A Chorus Line*, *42nd Street*, *The Music Man* and more. The songs, the choreography, the whole thing is just wonderful.

What a fun, comfortable, delicious day.

SATURDAY, DEC. 19

CRUISING TO MEMPHIS

I wake up realizing this is our final day of the cruise. Tomorrow, we disembark in Memphis and fly home. Sigh.

Today we cruise. No river town stops, just paddling along this blue and sparkling Mississippi. In the dining room, we share breakfast with two sisters—one from Michigan, the other from Arizona. The sister from Arizona is a school librarian, and, at ten in the Engine Room Bar, she says she'll be reading *The Cajun Night Before Christmas*.

We promise her we'll be there.

"That'll give me a chance to check out the engine room," Al says. "I've been wanting to do that all week long."

I mention that I checked it out and it was too hot for me, but that doesn't deter him. I suspect he'll be enthralled.

After breakfast, the two of us go out on deck as the *American Queen* glides under a bridge with her black stacks down. The day is clear, sunny, and cool. But with jackets on, it's comfortable. We watch the stacks rise back up after the boat clears the bridge. They glide back into place so smoothly it's almost like poetry.

"While you're in the engine room," I say, "I'm going to look at future cruises."

"Really?"

"Yes. This has been way too interesting a trip. I want to see what else is available."

"Well, be sure to check out cruises going down river," he says in between gulps of coffee. "If we take another of these cruises, I want more time for exploring on shore. No more abbreviated days because we're fighting a strong current."

The Engine Room Bar offers live music every night, following the last Grand Saloon show, but we're asleep long before the music starts.

This morning, as we enter the bar, we see about thirty-five people sitting in a half circle of comfortable wooden chairs and in the middle of the half circle, a tall, young man wearing a red Santa hat plays a serenely mellow cello. As the beautiful music flows effortlessly among us, I watch his long fingers gracefully shape each lovely note and wish I could create such aural wonder from wood and string. When I glance at the cellist's face, I'm surprised. I recognize him. He's Jeffrey from the Front Porch Cafe.

How many times has he helped me (and others) at the espresso machine? Who knew he was such an accomplished musician?

When he finishes his set and the applause dies down, I walk over and tell him how impressed I am. "You help me make my lattes in the morning, and I never knew you were a classical musician," I say. "Your music was fabulous."

He smiles, saying, "I have one more year at Loyola."

When the sisters enter, he quickly puts his cello in its case and leaves the room. I'm reminded how often I think I know someone because I see them doing their job. I think they're a teacher, or a waiter, or (like Jeffery) a barista, when, in reality, each person is so much more than they appear in our limited exposure to them.

I wish I'd known Jeffery was a musician and a college student studying music. I could have found some time to interview him about his work on the *American Queen* and his aspirations for the future. Opportunity lost.

The sister from Arizona takes her place in front of the half circle of chairs and the audience grows silent.

She opens a large book and begins to read us *The Cajun Night Before Christmas*. She reads with a full-throated Cajun accent and within moments we're captivated by this refreshing twist on an old, familiar classic.

The jolly old Saint Nick of this story, which takes place in a Louisiana bayou, is dressed all in muskrat. His skiff is full of toys and eight friendly alligators pull it along through the sky on its once-a-year mission.

The story and it's enthusiastic presentation are a hit with the Engine Room Bar crowd. There's laughter and applause and lots of friendly conversation when the story ends.

Al's Visit to the Engine Room

From my youth, I've been deeply attracted to machines that go whirr, which is to say: engines. The bigger and louder the better! I have a preschool memory of the coal-fired steam-powered freight train that ran near my grandparent's farm, a roaring monster that belched smoke and shook the ground. I was terrified. It was love at first sight.

My love for machines surely has a genetic component. My father, a steamship captain sailing the Pacific in the years before WWII, spoke of the black gang in the ship's engine room. The color was not a reference to their race, but to the coal dust covering them.

Engine rooms were places filled with swarthy men given to loud cursing, busily shoveling coal into the maw of mammoth boilers, tending to hot, greasy machinery which spouted steam and dripped oil. I was too little to be allowed to see it all, of course. Dangerous, *you know.*

I understood that this description might be a tad overstated, but Dad was a sailor and sailors have been known to prevaricate. In consequence, you will understand that when Sunny and I decided to cruise on the American Queen, *I was eager to see the boat's engine room.* B*ut the cruise has been so filled with interesting things to do, I haven't had a chance to check it out until today, the final day of our trip.*

I descend the metal stairs into the room where the power's made, and am surprised.

My, how times change. The Queen's *engine room, readily accessible from the Engine Room Bar at the back of the boat, was—is—an immaculate, orderly, and relatively quiet place. It is, as expected, rather warm and smells oily; the engine room crew's main job is to continually lubricate moving parts. There's a lot of machinery, and pipes, and valves, and stuff, all painted white.*

You could eat down here, though they'd be watching to make sure you took your dishware back upstairs.

You are welcome to take pictures or videos, or simply stand and watch the engine's pistons languidly going back and forth, turning the paddlewheel. The technician on duty, carefully monitoring gauges and indicators, gladly tells me about his steam engine and answers my questions. A handout is *available.*

The folks from American Queen *are obviously proud of their power plant, and rightly so. The engine itself has an interesting history. It was salvaged from a 1932 Corps of Engineers' dredge which had gone out of service and was sitting, forlorn and unused, in a Mississippi bayou. Newcastle Engineering rebuilt the engine. In the course of the rebuild, the engine's controls were automated, but it is otherwise just as it was first made. Now that engine runs the* American Queen.

I'm fond of saying, "Old Guys Rule." So do old steam engines!

Technically speaking, the power plant itself is (and I quote from an American Queen *handout) a "four-cylinder, horizontally inclined, tandem-piston, steeple-compounded, double-acting reciprocating" steam engine. I'll attempt to decipher this.*

There are four cylinders in the engine (think of your Toyota). These are arranged in pairs; one pair on each side of the paddlewheel. Each pair is physically connected together, or steeple compounded.

Live (fresh from the boiler) high-pressure steam enters the first cylinder and does its job (pushes a piston); then, somewhat-tired steam (at a lower pressure) enters the second cylinder and pushes another piston: that's tandem piston.

The steam is then condensed and returned as water back to the boiler, where it's turned back into steam and everything starts over. If you guess that this is a very efficient use of steam energy, you get a gold star.

You might ask: When the pistons get to the end of their travel, how do they get back to start over? That's easy: just reverse where the steam goes in. This makes the engine double-acting. Since that happens automatically and repeatedly, the engine is said to be reciprocating. Just like your Toyota.

Horizontally inclined is easy. The engine sits flat, distributing weight and keeping tall bits from poking into the cabin above, which would happen if the engine stood up.

This is, likely, a much more advanced plant than that found in the ships of my father's day. The swarthy coal shovelers of yesteryear are long gone, and though today's machinery is still hot and greasy, it's well-mannered. I was—and am—impressed.

You may now have a glass of something and congratulate yourself: you know how the Queen's *steam engine operates. If this is a tad too complex, just remember to pick up a copy of the engine room handout. You'll readily learn enough of the story to dazzle your friends even if you don't fully understand it. Remember what I said earlier: sailors are prone to prevarication.*

And so, enough technology. Time to head for fresh-baked peanut butter cookies!

* * *

While Al's exploring the Engine Room, I take the *American Queen* catalog out to the Front Porch and find a seat at an empty table. As we paddle toward Memphis, I go through the catalog page by page, reading all about the various cruises offered up and down the Mississippi and along the Ohio River.

Every cruise excites me. If we had enough money, I'd take them all. And I know Al would be just as eager for the experience. He'd be checking out the dessert menus and the photo opportunities at the various stops along the trip.

As I've mentioned, we're both travel enthusiasts. We love wandering with our cameras—and I with my note pad—to see what we can find. Whether it's a new city or a new neighborhood. A museum or a country path we've never walked before. We're especially fond of libraries and book stores, beaches and forests, old churches, and bakeries serving rich, hot coffee.

As I thumb through the catalog, my mind fills with scenes of river towns, of antebellum mansions surrounded by vast gardens, and other discoveries we've made on this trip. These are things I'd never seen before, except perhaps in books. But now I have a feel for them, as if I almost know them because I've walked among them, breathed the air around them, felt the mist or mystery within them while on this cruise.

Travel enriches us intellectually, emotionally, even physically. Research finds that traveling is good for our health. It stimulates our brains and exercises our bodies. It refreshes and renews us.

I know from personal experience that it enlarges my understanding. As Oliver Wendell Holmes, Jr. once said, "A mind that is stretched by a new experience can never go back to its old dimensions."

When I turn to the page in the catalog describing the Mark Twain-themed cruise from Minneapolis to St. Louis, my heart skips a beat. Here's a downstream cruise that includes lectures on Mark Twain's life and work. The boat will stop at towns in Minnesota, Wisconsin, Iowa, and Mark Twain's boyhood hometown: Hannibal.

Who wouldn't want to take this cruise focused on the most iconic American author of all times? Daily lectures about him, his life, and his work, and an opportunity to spend the day in his childhood hometown; it's a dream cruise on a dream boat.

When Al returns from the engine room, I show him the itinerary, and we make our way to the onboard sales desk, next to the Purser's Station.

Alex Stylianou, in charge of guest services and future cruise reservations, talks with us about the Mark Twain cruise. He offers us a significant and welcome discount because we're scheduling a cruise while on a cruise. And we give him a check. Hooray! We'll be back next August.

After a long, relaxed lunch in the dining room, we mosey to the Grand Saloon for Bobby

Durham's last River Chat. Today he's full of fun, giving us a glimpse of all the sayings that come from the history of river boating.

"You know the word *posh*, right? But do you know where it comes from? Well, back in the day when rich people cruised, they always wanted a room on the shore side of the boat. That's Port Out Starboard Home: POSH for short."

"Likewise, the term *high falutin'* came from wealthy passengers who wanted rooms near the beautiful stacks. The terms *blow his stack* and *letting off steam* come from river boating. The term *hell or high water* is a river-related term. Hell was when water was too low to travel. The phrase *hit a snag* is an old riverboat or flat boat phrase."

He tells stories and answers questions. He says our cruise, when it ends, will have covered six hundred forty river miles. And he ends his final talk with a song, accompanying himself on his banjo: "Riverboat Days." It's a great ending to what we've enjoyed for the past eight days.

Following a luxurious afternoon nap, we once again head for the Grand Saloon for the

Captain's Farewell Reception. The place is full and the Steamboat Syncopators are playing toe-tapping river songs when we arrive.

Phil Westbrook and Alex Bernhardt greet us by name as we enter. Each of them shakes our hands and makes us feel like old friends as they thank us for taking the cruise. We find two seats together amid the crowd, and claim them. Women with trays of champagne and egg rolls walk the aisles, offering refreshments. Within a few minutes, every Grand Saloon seat is full and passengers are still coming in. They stand along the walls with their glasses of champagne. We, and others who do not drink, are given ginger ale.

Captain Brent Willits with his trim goatee and his full-dress navy-blue uniform takes center stage and announces, "All good things must end."

A groan rises from the crowd. We don't want this cruise to end.

"But before we say goodbye, I want to let you know what I've loved about this cruise," he says. He pauses and then says, "The guests. You come from all different walks of life. Some of you are teachers, some scientists, some business people. But one thing you all have in common is that you have been successful. You have a great outlook on life. And that adds so much to our daily experience.

"I also treasure our staff and crew." At this the theater fills with cheers. All of us know full well how good this *American Queen* staff and crew has been. "The *American Queen* is the largest steamship in the world," he continues, "and our All-American staff and crew is the best, too."

He begins to call out the various staffs: housekeeping, the wait staff, the galley staff, and as he names them, they come running down the center aisle and up onto the stage. As they mount the stage, we're all cheering. Some of the men in the audience emit enthusiastic whistles.

When he calls the entertainment staff, the place goes wild. We've loved the evening shows and the talented, energetic folks who have entertained us so well.

Then Captain Willits lifts his glass and bids us "thank you" and farewell. We tip up our glasses, then the theater fills with applause and cheers as the staff people head out of the Grand Saloon.

Cruise Director Alex Bernhardt ends the gathering by singing “Old Man River.”

It has truly been a cruise to remember.

AL'S CONCLUSION ABOUT THIS CRUISE

(Written November 6, 2017)

It's hard to realize that almost two years have passed since we first voyaged on the American Queen. *We've been many places over that span of time, both here and across the Pond. In all our travels, though, the* American Queen *stands out, holding a special place in my mind—in our minds. Simply put, we haven't found anything or anywhere else that's quite like this Queen of the River.*

When my Dearly Beloved asked me to write what I felt about the voyage, what I liked, what I learned, I had to pause a few minutes.

Hmmm. Tough question. You're asking an old male to express his feelings?

But, actually, my answer is easy. Delighted. That's the word. I was delighted with the American Queen. *It had been a long time since I'd had one of those "Oooooh" moments that were common when I was a youngster. And there were a lot of "Oooohs" to be had aboard the* Queen. *There was always something new and interesting, and, yes, even wonderful to do and see. Wonderful's not an adjective I use often.*

Specifics. Let's talk about the boat. I've been in many museums, but never one that floated, much less moved upriver. To voyage on the American Queen *is to undertake a museum trip back to the nineteenth century, a fascinating time for this history buff.*

Being on its decks was almost a Matrix *moment: there I was, Mark Twain, teeth firmly clenched on my pipe, dodging sandbars.*

To walk the Queen's *decks, eyeing the channel markers as we chugged along; to smell the marshy towheads; to watch waterfowl take flight from floating snags, is to put oneself back into that almost-timeless history.*

You can—as I did—imagine yourself to be anyone. A Choctaw brave, paddling his canoe. De Soto, awed at what he'd discovered. A tug captain. Pick someone. Step into the Queen's *staterooms and you're back in the nineteenth century. Peek into the Gentlemen's Card Room and know you're in the lair of river gamblers.*

My experience was vastly enhanced by the fact that the American Queen *is a paddlewheel steamboat, powered by a real steam engine. None of this gas turbine Azipod thruster stuff. Down in the engine room for all to see is an authentic, salvaged four-cylinder "horizontally inclined tandem-piston, steeple-compounded, double-acting, reciprocating steam engine." I was impressed. No, I was thrilled.*

I could have spent hours watching the engine effortlessly spinning the paddle wheel, driving us upriver. Mesmerizing.

But there was much else to do. Eating, for example.

The Queen's *fare brought joy to my palate. dining room or Front Porch Cafe, both excellent.*

I regard dessert as a food group, eaten first if possible and in two servings in any event. The American Queen *was more than up to the task.*

Further, and to my great joy, the cookie locker was kept stocked round the clock, and was just a short jaunt down the hall from our room. I recommend the peanut butter. The oatmeal raisin was a hot second, with the sugar cookie not far behind.

The delight continued when it was time to go ashore. I'd never been in a small riverfront town, and the American Queen's *front office picked some winners to visit.*

It wasn't just the towns themselves, though; it was getting to and around in them. You don't know how much this matters to me. When someone says "Don't worry; he won't get far on foot," they may very well be referring to me with my arthritic knees and hip. A cruise on the Queen *includes a fleet of hop-on, hop-off buses at each port stop that let me see the sights and have enough energy left over to get back for a cookie. And a nap.*

What else? What have I learned? I guess I'd sum it up by saying that the land of the Mississippi is a special and unique place. The American Queen *not only introduced me to that unique land, it also made the introduction fun and— dare I say?—exciting.*

This was an extraordinary trip. We will definitely be back.

SUNNY'S AFTER-CRUISE COMMENTS

When we registered for this cruise, I looked forward to learning about the Mississippi and the river towns along its course. The second-longest river in the U.S. (after the Missouri River), the Mississippi has more historical importance than any other waterway in the country.

When our nation was young, it was the route of explorers, fur trappers, merchantmen, and scallywags. The river's role in the Civil War was central to its outcome. And today, the river is the lifeblood of commerce. Yet I knew very little about the Mississippi before this cruise. Thanks to Riverlorian Bobby Durham and his daily lectures, I know a lot more now.

I also looked forward to spending eight days on a floating work of art, and we certainly did that. From the polished, scrolling woodwork and antiques inside, to the rocking chairs on outside decks, we were immersed in Victorian–era opulence and enjoyed every moment of it.

Our bed was comfortable, our room a little gem, and the food, the service and the entertainment were all top-notch. We didn't have to don formal attire for dinner—a real plus in Al's opinion.

As I think of it now, there were a number of things besides formal nights missing from this cruise. For example, there was no casino. There were no children or teenagers. There were no photographers snapping our picture at dinner or the theater. There was no tiny fridge in the room—there wasn't space for one. This cruise gave us a comfortable, relaxing journey filled with beauty, and history, and gracious service.

I not only learned about the Mississippi River and its river towns, I also learned something about myself during this cruise. I discovered that I'd never thought very deeply about the antebellum mansions and the "genteel" lifestyle of the Old South. Never consciously connected it to the repugnant institution of slavery.

But after visiting gorgeous mansions and hearing about how wealthy the cotton farmers were, and after seeing shameful photos of slaves and masters in museum rooms dedicated to the Confederacy, my awareness woke up with a jolt.

Realizing that the "genteel" life was only possible because slaves performed all field and house labor, I found myself less enamored by antebellum mansions. Instead, my interest turned toward the slaves themselves. How in the world could they survive such an inhuman arrangement?

Looking back, I regret that I knew nothing about the Forks of the Road slave market in Natchez. Had I known about this pre-Civil War marketplace, I surely would have wanted to visit it. Should we ever return to Natchez, we'll make a point of spending time at this painful historic spot.

How could I have lived so long without recognizing the slave connection to the wealth and culture of the Old South? I don't know. But this cruise opened my eyes and expanded my heart.

And that's what travel can do. It enables us to grow in all sorts of ways. That growth, that personal development is one of the reasons I love to travel, and one of the reasons I encourage others to venture forth.

Of course, there are always surprises on a trip like this. Meeting Fred Bishop and learning about his link with my family was a uniquely special surprise for me!

My overall assessment: The cruise and this beautiful boat were amazing. I can't wait for the Mark Twain-themed cruise!

AUTHOR REQUEST

If you've enjoyed our book, please tell your friends about it. We appreciate when our readers spread the word online and in person. It's a great encouragement to us, and one of the few ways we have of letting other readers know about our books.

And if you have the time and are so inclined, please leave a reader review at Amazon or Goodreads or on your Facebook page.

Just go to our book's page at Amazon.com to leave your comments and ratings. To reach our book's page, simply type the title and our byline in the Amazon search bar.

Reader reviews help those searching online to find books they'd enjoy. And they keep our book visible.

Thank you.

ABOUT THE AUTHORS

Al and Sunny Lockwood have traveled by foot, car, rail, air and cruise ship. They've camped in national parks, hiked mountain trails, photographed springtime flowers in Death Valley and wintry surf along the rugged beaches of Northern California.

They've watched July Fourth fireworks over Lake Tahoe, explored the Taos Pueblo, and ridden the Great Smoky Mountains Railroad through forests ablaze with autumn colors.

They've ridden the amazing Falkirk Wheel in Scotland and the exciting Flam Railway in Norway.

And everywhere they go, they capture unforgettable moments—Al with his camera and Sunny with her reporter's notebook. In addition to their travel memoirs, their work has been published in magazines and newspapers. It has been recognized with awards from the National Federation of Press Women, the California Newspaper Publishers Association, the Seven Sisters Book Awards, The Wishing Shelf Book Awards, the National Indie Excellence Awards and the Best Book Awards.

Taken in an Athens coffee shop, when Al and Sunny ducked inside to escape a sudden downpour.

You can contact the Lockwoods at:
sunnyandallockwood@gmail.com

OTHER TRAVEL MEMOIRS

BY AL & SUNNY LOCKWOOD

Cruising Panama's Canal
Savoring 5,000 nautical miles and 500,000 decadent calories

Cruising the Mediterranean
From the luminous canals of Amsterdam and Venice to the stunning mosaics of Istanbul's Blue Mosque, this travel memoir takes readers on the trip of a lifetime.

Finding Ourselves in Venice, Florence, Rome & Barcelona
Aging adventurers discover the power of place while exploring fascinating cities at their own relaxing pace

Cruising the Atlantic
Our Epic journey from Barcelona to Miami

Printed in Great Britain
by Amazon

80564277R00108